THE SCHOOL MENTOR HANDBOOK

THE SCHOOL MENTOR HANDBOOK

Essential skills and strategies for working with student teachers

Hazel Hagger, Katharine Burn and Donald McIntyre

KOGAN
PAGE

Ringbinder edition first published in 1993
Reprinted 1993 (twice), 1994 (twice)
This paperback edition published in 1995

Kogan Page Limited
120 Pentonville Road
London N1 9JN

British Library Cataloguing in Publication Data

A CIP record for this book is available from the British Library.

ISBN 0 7494 1601 7

Typeset by DP Photosetting, Aylesbury, Bucks
Printed and bound in Great Britain by
Biddles Ltd, Guildford and King's Lynn

Contents

ACKNOWLEDGEMENTS

This Handbook is based on the work of the Oxford Internship Scheme. All those who are partners in that scheme, in Oxfordshire secondary schools, Oxfordshire LEA, and the University of Oxford, have directly or indirectly contributed to its production. Our thanks go especially to all the mentors who allowed themselves to be observed and interviewed, or who commented on early drafts of these materials, in order that their hard-won expertise could be used in the hope of making the task easier for others. We drew especially heavily on the time, understanding and guidance of members of our Steering Committee – Carol Minshall and Geoff Rhodes, who were also invaluable consultants, and Anna Pendry, Terry Allsop and Richard Pring. To them, and most of all to Judith Lathlean, who conducted all the investigations with care, thoughtfulness and intelligence, must go much of the credit for the production of this Handbook; and we are very grateful to them.

Hazel Hagger
Katharine Burn
Donald McIntyre

PREFACE TO PAPERBACK EDITION

When *The School Mentor Handbook* was first published in 1993, it was produced in a loose-leaf form. The intention was that a school or department would be able to photocopy those parts of it which different members of staff wanted to use. Sales and other feedback suggest that up to now the Handbook has been used, and found useful, in that way by about a thousand schools. However, it has also become increasingly clear that individual mentors and other teachers would welcome their own copies of the Handbook in the convenient form of a paperback book and at a realistic price for individual buyers. We are delighted that Kogan Page has therefore agreed to publish this paperback edition. Its availability in this form will we hope enhance its practical usefulness as a handbook for mentors. In addition, we believe that it will also facilitate teachers' study and discussion of the ideas about mentoring which it offers.

The work of school-based initial teacher education is still in its very early stages and we all have much to learn about it. We have found from experience that the ideas presented in this Handbook, when discussed by groups of teachers in the light of their own experiences as mentors, provide a very fruitful basis for creative thinking as well as for straightforward learning. We hope therefore that this paperback edition will be a useful resource for school-based mentor discussion groups and for courses on mentoring, as it is in our own Oxford University Postgraduate Diploma in Mentoring.

We believe that this Handbook offers a guide to the best current practice in mentoring, and also a stimulus to thinking about how mentoring can be developed.

INTRODUCTION

SCHOOL-BASED INITIAL TEACHER EDUCATION

Throughout the last century, teachers' initial professional education has been based mainly in colleges and universities. Schools have had no formal obligation to participate in it and no significant influence on the policies which have shaped it. They have simply been places to which student teachers have been sent for 'teaching practice'; and the part played by teachers in the schools has been variable, generally subsidiary, often ambiguous and on a voluntary basis.

All this has now changed. Gradually and unevenly the universities and colleges recognized the need for schools and teachers to play a fuller and clearer part in initial teacher education; and in some cases they developed stronger partnerships with schools for this purpose. Then, in 1992, the government decided that initial teacher education for secondary teachers should be *predominantly* school-based; and this was followed up in 1993 with a similar, if not quite so radical, shift towards school-based initial teacher education for primary teachers.

There are very good reasons why this should happen. It has been clear all along to those who thought about it that the complex practical work of classroom teaching was not something that could be learned by first learning theoretical ideas and then simply putting them into practice. Learning what ideas are worth putting into practice, what ideas it is possible to put into practice, and under what circumstances any particular ideas are useful are all dependent upon experience in schools. Indeed, learning what it means to be a school-teacher can only be learned in schools. Furthermore, it is only in schools that the expertise of school-teaching is daily being practised and is available for the novice to learn from. As successive generations of student teachers have known, it is mainly from teachers and in schools that the practical arts of teaching can best be learned.

The case for the major contribution to initial teacher education being made by schools and practising teachers is then, at least in broad outline, a very obvious one. The case which needs to be made is instead that for the involvement of universities and colleges. That case too, however, although less obvious, is a very strong one. Without university and college courses, the *range* of valuable and practical educational ideas which student teachers would learn would generally be much more limited and more arbitrarily selective than it has been in recent years. Without university and college courses, the quality of the thinking which student teachers would develop as professional educators would be likely to be more limited, with important kinds of arguments about good practice being relatively neglected and not effectively learned. Further- more, any adequate initial teacher education programme which did not make use of the economies of scale that courses in higher education institutions allow would as a result be prohibitively expensive. These and other points about the contributions which higher education institutions should make to initial teacher education will not be developed here: that is not what this Handbook is about. It should be understood, however, that the enthusiasm for school-based teacher education which underlies this Handbook does not imply any lack of enthusiasm for the equally important contribution necessary from higher education institu- tions.

The strongest argument for the shift towards more school-based teacher education is the neglect over the last century of the expertise of practising experienced teachers: embedded in the day-to-day work of virtually every school in the country there is a rich mine of expertise which should be drawn upon in the professional education of each new generation of teachers. It is through taking account of the nature of this expertise that we can best think about how initial teacher education can be improved by making it more school-based. Four characteristic features of teaching expertise seem to be:

- Practicality.
  A constant concern of teachers has to be with what is possible, what is feasible, what is likely to work within the practical constraints under which they teach:

    - the number and diversity of the pupils in a class

    - the time available for any lesson or any given topic

    - the quantity and nature of the resources available

    - the criteria and procedures by which the pupils are to be assessed

    - the amount of noise that a particular approach would involve

    - the need for whatever is done to be orderly and not to endanger pupils' safety.

- Contextualized judgement.
  A related characterization of teacher expertise is its dependence on knowledge of aspects of the particular context in which one is working; what to try to achieve on any occasion and how to set about it depends on a knowledge of such things as:

- the particular class and its recent history

- particular pupils in the class

- their morale, mood, energy, enthusiasm, interests and attainments

- the ways in which things are done in this school

- what materials are available and where and how they can be found

- one's own expertise, energy and confidence.

■ Fluency.
Experienced teachers are generally able to conduct their classroom teaching with flexibility, effectiveness and remarkable fluency. In the course of their teaching they make many complex judgements about what to do, taking account of a great deal of information, and do so almost instantaneously. This marvellous fluency, which experienced teachers themselves tend to take for granted, not recognizing the complexity of what they are doing, can make teaching look misleadingly easy to novices.

■ Idiosyncrasy.
While there is much that experienced teachers generally agree about as being necessary for good teaching, there are also many variations in their ways of doing things. Teachers vary in what they value and therefore in what they emphasize in their teaching; in addition, teachers each have their different repertoires of ways of acting to achieve similar ends.

Such is the expertise that seems necessary for effective classroom teaching. There are perhaps two important inferences which can be drawn.

A different kind of expertise

The expertise of experienced teachers is strikingly different in nature from the academic knowledge which can be offered by universities and colleges. Whereas the former is practical, contextualized, implicit in teachers' practice and varies with the individual, the latter is often idealized, is necessarily generalized across contexts and aims to be as explicit and as objective as possible.

This suggests that it would be foolish to think of the move towards school-based teacher education as a takeover by the schools of what the colleges used to do. There is no reason to believe that the schools are well-placed to do the work that was previously done by the colleges. What the schools can do is complement the work of the colleges by making accessible to student teachers their own different and at least equally important expertise, which until now they have not had the opportunity to offer effectively.

The importance of this point can hardly be exaggerated. Since all our images of initial teacher education have been learned in a college-dominated system, the temptation for teachers to model themselves on what college lecturers do is very strong. Yet this would be missing the opportunity to do the important job which only they can do.

Developing new teacher-educator skills

If school-based teacher-educators are not simply to copy the practices of college-based teacher-educators, they will need to develop new skills of their own, using their own distinctive expertise. It would be a mistake to think that this will be an easy task.

The characteristic features, outlined above, of teacher expertise give some indication of the difficulty of developing teacher-educator skills based on one's expertise as a classroom teacher. In that this expertise emphasizes what is practical, how does it relate to the visions of teaching which have drawn student teachers to the profession? In that it is highly contextualized, of what generalizable value can it be to a student teacher? In that it is idiosyncratic, why should a student teacher pay any attention to how one individual sets about the task of teaching? Most of all, in that experienced teachers' expertise is *invisible*, embedded and implicit in their practice, how can a student teacher gain access to it and so learn from it? It is perhaps because clear answers have not been given to these questions that experienced teachers' expertise has been so neglected in initial teacher education until now.

A growing body of research is demonstrating that without clear answers to these questions, school-based teacher education which relies on established common sense and vague hopes that expertise will somehow 'rub off' on to student teachers will be anything but an improvement on previous practice. There is no doubt about the potential value of experienced teachers' expertise to student teachers. Furthermore, the one-to-one teacher-student ratio which teachers will generally have with their student teachers is one which opens up rich possibilities. Yet there will need to be thoughtful planning and careful evaluation of the approaches to be used if school-based teacher education is to realize its potential. This Handbook is the outcome of attempts over several years to engage in such planning and evaluation.

THE DEVELOPMENT OF THE HANDBOOK

In 1986 a group of teachers in Oxfordshire secondary schools, representatives of the Local Education Authority and tutors in the Department of Educational Studies at the University of Oxford, came together to work out how they could most effectively collaborate to develop a high quality initial teacher education course. The starting point for this work was a set of principles derived from research and experience of the problems and possibilities in initial teacher education. The thinking, planning and arguments went on for a whole year. the school-focused PGCE programme that they devised – the Oxford Internship Scheme – has been in operation since 1987. In its details the programme is, of course, designed to satisfy local conditions and circumstances, but the ideas and principles at the heart of the scheme are applicable to courses beyond Oxfordshire. In Australia, for example, a highly successful BEd Primary course has since been developed on the same principles.

Central to these ideas and principles is a very simple notion. In initial teacher education, people in schools should do what people in schools are best placed to do: namely, take advantage of the distinctive knowledge and expertise that they use on a day-to-day basis, and capitalize on the fact that they are in daily contact with the classes in which student teachers begin to practise teaching. Given the opportunity, student teachers themselves recognize how much teachers have to offer them. As part of a study of what and how they had learned from experienced teachers, a group of 30 randomly selected student teachers in the Oxford Internship Scheme were interviewed towards the end of their course. The list that follows is a compilation of their answers to the question: what knowledge do experienced teachers have that is valuable for learner teachers?

- experience

- organization

- awareness of realities, practicalities, constraints

- classroom control

- dealing with individuals

- knowing when to step in

- management of practical lessons

- small practical things that can make a difference to the smooth running of a lesson

- ways of organizing a classroom and pupils

- opening routines

- building habits with classes

- tried and tested strategies for handling different situations

- knowing how to turn academic knowledge into lesson content that makes sense to the pupils

- phasing of work to suit movement in the classroom

- timing of a lesson

- different ways of dealing with disruption

- knowing what's going on and how to change tack

- coping with anything that happens

- developed ways of interpreting what goes on and being able to respond quickly to classroom events

- marking and assessing

- pitching work appropriately for pupils of different abilities

- knowing how a lesson is going

- knowledge of:

  - curriculum

  - school

  - pupils

  - teachers

  - particular pupils

  - particular classes

  - classrooms

  - groups and how they can react.

In writing this Handbook we have made full use of the expertise, knowledge, thinking and experience of mentors within the Oxford Internship Scheme who have had the opportunity to develop ways of working with student teachers and to practise mentoring within a school-focused course since 1987. In 1991 a research and development project was set up to find out just how mentors were going about their work with student teachers. A research officer worked in schools, observing mentors, talking with them about the various tasks involved in mentoring, and getting their accounts of the different ways in which they worked as mentors. The many and diverse ways the mentors worked with their student teachers provided the researcher with a wealth of fascinating material which was used as the basis of a handbook for mentors and professional tutors working within the Oxford Internship Scheme.

We have drawn extensively on those materials produced for the Internship Scheme. However, in order to produce a Handbook that would be useful to mentors and their colleagues in as wide a range of circumstances as possible, we have edited, adapted and extended the materials rather than simply reproduced them. Furthermore, we have taken careful account of investigations of the work of mentors in other contexts. This Handbook is thus based on our view of what teachers generally can effectively and usefully offer to novices.

ROLES AND RESPONSIBILITIES

As people gradually come to terms with school-based initial teacher education, it is inevitable that there will be diverse views as to precisely what roles are needed, and also about appropriate titles for these roles. As we all gain more experience of it, however, and as more research is done, four things are becoming ever more clear:

The need for whole-school commitment

Becoming involved in school-based initial teacher education is an important step for any school to take. Unless it is a carefully considered undertaking, acceptance of responsibility for student teachers can distract teachers from their primary responsibility for their pupils and it can be a source of irritation for other members of staff. Properly planned, on the other hand, school-based teacher education can be highly beneficial for both pupils and teachers, as well as for the student teachers themselves; but this will happen only if it is clearly recognized as a whole-school commitment.

The critical question to be asked of the school as a whole is whether or not it provides a good learning environment for student teachers. Are they made welcome in the school? Is their ignorance about appropriate behaviour forgiven, and their enthusiasm to become teachers reinforced? Are they encouraged to see teaching as a complex and intriguing task about which one can usefully go on learning throughout a long career? Are members of staff all pleased to share their own distinctive expertise with the student teachers, either as part of a planned programme or informally? Do teachers see sufficient benefits for the school in taking on this task for them to be willing to accept new arrangements, and to learn the new skills and strategies that will be needed for it? Unless positive answers can be given to these questions *for the school as a whole*, it is very unlikely that either the school or the student teachers will find the experience rewarding.

The role of professional tutor

Headteachers themselves need to lead schools in being committed to making initial teacher education an integral part of the school's work. They will normally, however, need to delegate to another member of the senior management team the task of managing the whole school's engagement in teacher education. In secondary schools, that person is often called the *professional tutor*. Among the professional tutor's tasks are likely to be those of co-ordinating the school's involvement in initial teacher education, induction of student teachers into the school as a whole, arranging for them to gain experience of pastoral work, and organizing a programme of seminars and workshops on whole-school issues. The professional tutor will also probably have a role in leading the school's team of *mentors* from subject departments. In this Handbook we assume that normal good practice is for student teachers' learning about classroom teaching to be managed by a subject-specialist mentor. This Handbook concentrates on those aspects of mentoring used in helping student teachers to develop as classroom practitioners. (The skills and strategies needed by professional tutors are addressed in *The Management of Student Teachers' Learning*, which complements this Handbook for mentors.)

The role of mentor

The mentor is the person in the school with responsibility for managing and co-ordinating the student teacher's learning as it relates to subject teaching. It is most of all for mentors that this Handbook is intended. Much of the student teacher's learning is likely to be through working directly with mentors; and all the sections of this Handbook should therefore be useful for mentors. However, mentors are not the only experienced classroom teachers with whom student teachers work. The role of mentor not only includes helping student teachers directly in the mentor's classroom, but – at least equally important – supporting and coordinating subject colleagues in *their* work with student teachers. Chapter 1 of this Handbook is therefore of special and distinctive importance for the work of mentors.

The need for whole-department involvement

Student teachers in school subject departments usually spend time with several different classes, in the classrooms of the teachers who normally teach them. This diversity of experience is in itself a very important part of school-based teacher training. It is also very important, however, that student teachers should benefit as fully as possible from the expertise and insights of the different teachers with whom they work; there is something badly wrong if, for example, they are treated as learners in the mentor's classroom but merely as visitors, or as supply teachers, in other teachers' classrooms. Furthermore, most experienced teachers tend to be very ready to share their expertise with student teachers. A crucial need in school-based teacher training, therefore, is for careful arrangements to be made to ensure that all members of a subject department

- understand the teacher education scheme in which the school is participating

- are asked to undertake roles which are realistic in relation to their other commitments

-    are clear about the roles which they are being asked to play

-    have regular opportunities to compare notes with mentors about student teachers' progress

-    have opportunities to develop skills and strategies for working with student teachers such as those presented in this Handbook.

The mentor's role within a subject department is thus a demanding one: not only does the mentor have a special responsibility to develop the expertise necessary for promoting student teachers' learning; he or she also needs to lead and to coordinate the work of colleagues as they contribute to the student teachers' development.

If the head of department is not the mentor, then he or she also is a key person in establishing and sustaining the necessary professional commitment of the whole department. Heads of department can show their active support of the work with student teachers both by the way they themselves work with them and by allocating departmental time for the discussion of issues concerning initial teacher education. The head of department can greatly enhance the value of the mentor's work by ensuring that initial professional education is seen as the collective responsibility of the whole department.

How to use this handbook

A REFERENCE BOOK – NOT A TRAINING MANUAL

Partnership in initial teacher training recognizes that teachers, as mentors, have a critical role to play in the training of new entrants to the profession. However, the fact that you have considerable and invaluable expertise rooted in classroom practice does not mean that you will necessarily find it easy to pass on your skills and knowledge to student teachers. Teaching is a complex craft and this makes learning to teach very demanding. Enabling student teachers to learn from your own practice is challenging, especially if they are to be critical learners and not merely clones. It would be demeaning to the teaching profession to imply that mentoring was easy – simply an extension of your work as a teacher of school pupils.

The Handbook is not a training manual, in that there are no exercises to work through. Each unit explains a different aspect of the mentoring role, and needs first to be read as a whole; you can then refer back to it as and when you need to, selecting those ideas which you can usefully apply. You may then find the checklists and examples of proformas valuable both for your own work with student teachers, and in helping your colleagues in their work with them.

The ideas and suggested strategies within each unit can also form the basis of mentor induction and development through joint meetings of mentors within a partnership scheme – mentors either from a range of subject areas working in a single school, or from one subject area working with a particular university/college.

THE PRINCIPLES ON WHICH IT IS BASED

These materials are intended to be useful to mentors working within a wide variety of teacher training schemes. However, since they have been developed from the experience of mentors in one particular scheme, they inevitably rest on certain underlying assumptions. To use these materials effectively you will need to understand these assumptions even if they do not hold true in your particular scheme.

Partnership

We have assumed that mentors will be working as partners with university/ college tutors in the training of student teachers. You do not therefore carry sole responsibility for the student teachers and will have entered into a partnership agreement that sets out exactly what the contribution of mentors and tutors to the scheme is to be. Such an agreement is likely to recognize that what you as mentors are best placed to contribute is your own classroom expertise and understanding – knowledge rooted in practice. The materials here therefore focus on ways of helping student teachers learn from classroom practice through observation, discussion and experience. The university/college tutors will have other kinds of knowledge to contribute – based on research literature and awareness of professional practices elsewhere. These are not your responsibility, although you do have a role to play in helping student teachers reflect on and evaluate the different perspectives.

The assumption of a partnership does not mean that these materials will not prove useful to those mentors working in schools that have sole responsibility for initial teacher education. However, it should be recognized that they do not cover those aspects of teacher training which we consider to fall within the sphere of university/college tutors.

Progression: two phases in student teachers' learning

The aim of any initial teacher training course is to produce not merely competent teachers, but professionals who will continue to think critically about their teaching and continue to develop and refine their teaching skills. To help student teachers acquire basic competence and to enable them to build up the skills and attitudes necessary for such self-evaluation, the Oxford Internship Scheme adopted a model of teacher training which falls into two distinct phases. In the first phase student teachers' learning is focused on an agreed list of skills, qualities and abilities and their progress is assessed in relation to these. The second phase begins when, in the opinion of mentor and university tutor, they have shown themselves to be competent teachers. During this second phase, confident in their own ability, they are able to begin to articulate their own goals as teachers and to develop the criteria by which to evaluate their own teaching. Having achieved the standard of basic competence, they are able to take much more responsibility for directing their own learning. Although many partnership schemes may not *formally* recognize these two distinct phases, our experience has shown that as student teachers acquire basic competence so their learning can be fruitfully developed by strategies that depend upon self-evaluation.

ASPECTS OF MENTORING: THE SEQUENCE OF UNITS

The first unit, Classroom Practice: Planning and Coordinating the Student Teachers' Learning in School, is concerned with the management responsibilities of the mentor's role. However, in order to manage student teachers' learning in school effectively it is important to consider how the student teachers will learn. This unit therefore explores in detail the needs of beginning teachers and the issues you will have to consider in devising and implementing an effective programme for them. It should be read first, partly because the issues it addresses – like the need for a protected introduction and gradual progression in the student teachers' programme – will inform your selection of strategies to use at any particular time, and partly because it sets out the kind of preparation you will need to do before the student teachers even arrive in school, whether for their first or final placement.

A gradual introduction to classroom teaching means that student teachers, when they first come into school, will naturally spend some time observing. For this reason the second unit is on Observation. However, it is important that student teachers do not abandon observation once they begin teaching. Research has shown that observation continues to be useful to student teachers after they have begun to develop the skills of classroom teaching themselves. They then have a clearer grasp of what it is they need to learn, are better placed to recognize what is going on in the classroom and are more able to ask questions about what they see in order to understand what you are doing and why. For this reason we have included a second unit relating to the observation of experienced teachers' practice. Unit 5, Opening up Your Practice, explains ways in which you can help student teachers gain maximum benefit from observation and post-lesson discussion.

Unit 3, Assessment and Supervision, is critical to the student teachers' learning since this is the means by which you provide regular feedback on their teaching, assess their progress in relation to your agreed list of teaching competences, and help them set new targets for their future learning. However, in the second phase of the student teachers' learning – when they have shown themselves to be competent teachers – your role in diagnostic assessment and supervision changes to one of supporting their own self-evaluation. It is because this emphasis on self-evaluation clearly belongs to the second phase of the student teachers' learning, a phase which they are likely to enter nearer the end of the course than the beginning, that this forms the last unit in the book. Units 3 and 7 are the only two units which fall into this kind of chronological sequence and your use of them will therefore vary depending on the progress of the student teacher and on what stage of their course you are working with them in school.

Unit 4 focuses on collaborative teaching, a lesson taught jointly by you and a student teacher. Like observation, collaborative teaching is likely to be a strategy that you will use early in the student teachers' training as a means of providing a gentle introduction to classroom teaching. Student teachers can begin to practise some of the skills of teaching without having to take full responsibility for a whole class. However, because collaborative teaching also provides opportunities for student teachers to learn from the planning and classroom practice of the teacher they are working with, this too can provide a valuable means of learning throughout the student teachers' time in school.

Critically Discussing Student Teachers' Ideas – Unit 6 – also obviously has a place in your work with student teachers when they first come in to school. It is important for you, when you begin working with them, to discover something about their preconceptions and ideas about teaching. Understanding the ideas they bring with them will help you in providing an appropriate programme for them. However, throughout their training it is also important that they are encouraged to reflect upon and critically evaluate ideas that they bring with them from the university/college elements of their course. Thus, critically evaluating their ideas is a skill you will need to use whenever the student teachers come to you and throughout their time in school.

With the exception of Units 3 and 7, there is no chronological ordering of the skills and strategies that you will use. It is sensible to start with the unit on Classroom Practice: Planning and Coordinating the Student Teachers' Learning in School, but the other units will be useful to you in different ways at whatever stage in their training the student teachers come to you.

The structure of the units

Each unit follows a broadly similar pattern and includes:

- a definition of the particular skill or way of working with student teachers

- a rationale explaining how the particular process can contribute to the student teachers' learning

- suggestions of ways in which the process can be most effectively carried out

- an analysis of the difficulties that you may encounter in implementing the strategy, and suggestions about how these may be overcome

- suggestions of ways in which you can support your colleagues in their work with the student teachers

- planning sheets, observation records and checklists which you and your colleagues can use in working with student teachers

- a summary of the main points.

All the units are based on research into the work of experienced mentors. They are therefore illustrated throughout with examples and comments from those mentors – examples and comments that reflect the reality of mentoring in the pressured environment of busy schools. We hope that their experiences and insights will prove useful to you in your work with student teachers.

CLASSROOM PRACTICE: PLANNING AND COORDINATING THE STUDENT TEACHERS' LEARNING IN SCHOOL

Classroom teaching is so complex and demanding that student teachers' learning cannot be left to chance. Planning of their learning is, therefore, essential. A significant part of the student teachers' learning will result directly from working with you, but you will also need to draw on the classes, expertise and perspectives of other teachers. Managing the student teachers' learning in school involves not only working closely with the student teachers, but also helping your colleagues to work effectively with them as well.

KEY CONSIDERATIONS

In school you have overall responsibility for enabling your student teachers to:

- acquire classroom competency

- carry out any school-based tasks from the programme devised by the university/college and the school in partnership

- test ideas and develop their own thinking about the kind of teachers they want to become.

To manage your student teachers' learning effectively, your work with them needs to be guided by the following considerations.

Progression

Your expectations of student teachers, the opportunities you offer them, and the demands you make of them will vary depending on their level of experience, the progress they have made, and their familiarity with the school. A student teacher in his or her first week in a school will obviously need a different programme from that designed for a confident and competent student nearing the end of their training.

The programme should be structured enough to allow development and progression, but flexible enough to accommodate change. This will leave you to judge, for example, when to shift the balance of activities from observation to collaborative teaching, or from working with individuals and small groups to taking responsibility for a whole class.

Protection

Student teachers are likely to learn faster and more effectively if their first experiences in the classroom are positive ones. In the words of an experienced mentor:

> The start is important. They shouldn't be chucked in at the deep end; they should be given time to progress from sound, positive experiences in the classroom.

In their first weeks in school it is advisable for them to work with individuals and small groups rather than whole classes, to work alongside you and other experienced teachers rather than on their own, and to have contact with classes that are not perceived as especially 'difficult' to teach.

Importance of working with a mentor

It is vital that you are able to work with the student teachers in the classroom for sufficient time to build a constructive working relationship with them and to be able to monitor and evaluate their progress with confidence.

A timetabled weekly mentor period away from the classroom is an important element in the student teachers' programme. It provides the opportunity to plan ahead, allocate tasks for the coming days/week, and draw the student teachers into evaluative discussions of all that they have seen and done during the week.

Colleagues

There are limits to what you can provide for your student teachers with your own classes, teaching and thinking. On a practical level you simply do not have the time to provide them with all the experiences they need in school. Moreover, there is always the danger of 'cloning' for any student teacher who works exclusively with one teacher. The more that student teachers experience a range of teaching skills, styles and perspectives, the less likely they are to ape unquestioningly what they see. Working with a range of teachers can also help student teachers feel involved in the work of a department/faculty and at home in the school.

Before colleagues start working with the student teachers it is important that they understand what such work will involve. As mentor, whatever your position in the department or faculty, you are responsible for ensuring that colleagues working with the student teachers:

- are realistic and do not expect the student teachers to be 'super-teachers' from day one

- understand the nature and principles of the school-based scheme you are operating

- are kept fully informed of the student teachers' programme and progress

- are supported in their work with student teachers and helped to develop the skills needed for this work.

The problems and challenges of involving colleagues can be seen in the observations of two experienced mentors.

EXAMPLE Negotiating with colleagues

'In my first year as a mentor I drew up the student's timetable to fit in with what my colleagues wanted. The poor thing ended up teaching a lot of very difficult groups. The following year I took the trouble to sit down with all of them and negotiated a much more balanced timetable.'

EXAMPLE Shared understandings

'Before the student teachers arrive I make sure that everyone in the department understands how to work with them and that we're all clued up about things like collaborative teaching and diagnostic assessment. I see this as a real priority after the mess a couple of years ago when I discovered that one of my colleagues simply left the student teacher to get on with it and hadn't seen her teach for six weeks. I also make sure that working with student teachers is an item at every departmental meeting.'

Student teachers as adult learners

Student teachers are in a peculiar position in school. They are adults but they are learners. As adults they all have a history behind them, and many arrive in school with a wealth of experience and expertise in other fields. They are unlikely, however, to have any knowledge of the school and its workings. Not knowing the intricacies of the staffroom coffee arrangements does not make them thoroughly inadequate and ignorant.

Any newcomer to the school – especially someone in the insecure position of a student teacher – needs to understand how the school works, from such things as the structure of the pastoral system to who sits where in the staffroom. In addition, student teachers need to know what is expected of them, even down to such details as how they should address the headteacher and what is the accepted standard of dress for teachers in that school. For them to feel secure in the school and in their learning they also need to have a clear idea of what they are going to be doing from one week to the next.

Time spent talking with your student teacher(s) about the training programme and the ways in which you will be working with them is a good investment. Sometimes problems can occur simply because you and the student teacher(s) have never discussed the ways in which you will be working together in school. The experiences of an established Modern Languages mentor illustrate the point very well.

EXAMPLE Avoiding misunderstandings – talking about ways of working

The mentor found John (the student teacher) very difficult to work with. He contributed little or nothing to collaborative planning, had nothing to say following observation of the mentor, and generally seemed apathetic. When the mentor explained her concern to him about his lack of progress it became clear that he thought that all the things she set up for him were a waste of time. 'He insisted that the only way to learn to teach was to be left to get on with it alone behind closed doors. It took me some time to convince John that diving in at the deep end wasn't a good idea for either him or the pupils. In the end he did quite well, but we lost three or four weeks of valuable time because in a way we were talking at cross-purposes. Now talking about how they're going to learn is part of the induction programme.'

Once student teachers have settled into the school it is easy to forget that they are not experienced teachers. As beginners they need to take a long time in planning and evaluating lessons; they have no store of past lessons to tap in to. It is tempting to give them a fullish teaching timetable, arguing that they need to know what it is like to be a real teacher. The demands of learning to teach – planning thoroughly, learning from other teachers, learning through reading and discussion, acquiring classroom teaching skills, thinking about the kind of teachers they want to become, learning how to evaluate their work and exploring whole-school issues – are exhausting enough.

Being realistic

In drawing up programmes for your student teacher(s) you will have to take account of a number of needs, constraints and interests. You have to give consideration to the learning needs of your pupils as well as those of the student teachers, the interests and views of colleagues, the availability of classes on the days/weeks when the student teachers are in school, and the needs of your department and school. This is a tall order. It is not always possible to satisfy everyone and compromises have to be reached. Moreover, your own teaching commitments mean that you cannot necessarily always give the time to your student teacher(s) that you would like to and feel they deserve. Feeling guilty is counter-productive. As one mentor wryly commented:

> I'm not much of an example to newcomers to the profession if I'm late for my lessons because I'm spending too much time with them. There's always loads to talk about between lessons but sometimes five minutes is all you have time for and five minutes is better than nothing.

PLANNING AND PREPARATION AT DIFFERENT STAGES

The following checklists are by no means exhaustive. They are intended to alert you to the key issues involved in planning an effective programme for student teachers at different stages in their training.

CHECKLIST Preparing for the arrival of the student teachers in school

- Liaise with the person responsible for departmental meetings so that working with student teachers can become a regular agenda item.

- Ensure that all teachers who will be working with the student teachers understand their legal responsibilities.

- Try to guide colleagues in their work with student teachers by passing on (and discussing with them) any relevant materials concerning initial teacher education produced by the partners in the scheme.

- Discuss with colleagues how student teachers are to be introduced to classes (it is important that their status is not undermined).

- Alert colleagues to the range of ways in which they might usefully work with student teachers, including:

  - discussion with student teachers prior to a lesson so they know the teacher's initial plans

  - structured observation of experienced teachers in action

  - discussing with student teachers the actions which they took and the decisions which they made in lessons

  - enabling student teachers to practise those same skills in part of a lesson in a 'protected' way

  - giving student teachers feedback on that practice

  - joint lesson planning for future lesson(s)

  - collaborative teaching so that student teachers have some responsibility in the classroom but in a 'protected' way

  - enabling student teachers to take full responsibility for a single lesson or series of lessons

  - discussing critically with the student teachers the ideas they have been exploring elsewhere.

- If and when available, read the student application forms for the course to get to know their backgrounds and get some 'feel' for their interests and needs.

- Familiarize yourself with any school tasks that are part of a programme planned jointly with the university/college so that you can enable them to be accomplished.

continued overleaf

- Draw up a detailed plan for inducting the student teacher(s) into your department.

- Liaise with the professional tutor to ensure there is no overlap between whole-school and departmental induction programmes.

- Make sure that everyone is clear about student teacher access to photocopying and other resources.

- Consult colleagues and gain approval for the programme which you devise for the first few weeks of the student teachers' school-based experience so that both colleagues and student teacher(s) know in advance what they will be doing.

Induction – the school as a whole

In many secondary schools the professional tutor will take responsibility for the induction of student teachers into the school as a whole, with the mentor responsible for departmental/faculty induction. The student teachers' first day in the school is very important, but it should be seen as part of a structured programme aiming to introduce and gradually integrate them into the ethos and workings of the school.

A typical first whole-school induction day might look like this:

	8.40	Professional tutor meets student teachers on their arrival.
Tutor time	8.45 – 9.00	Cloakroom facilities and base for the day pointed out. Distribution of copies of the school handbook and the day's programme.
Period I	9.00 – 9.30	Meet the headteacher.
	9.30 – 9.45	Meet office staff.
	9.45 – 10.00	Meet resources staff and school librarian.
Period II	10.00 – 11.00	Tour of school with senior pupils as guides (student teachers with maps).
Break	11.00 – 11.20	Coffee with subject mentors.
Period III	11.20 – 12.20	Shadowing a pupil in Year 9.
Lunch	12.20 – 12.50	Lunch in school canteen with professional tutor and mentor.
	12.50 – 1.15	Staffroom with professional tutor and mentor.
Period IV	1.20 – 2.20	Continue shadowing Year 9 pupil.
Period V	2.20 – 3.20	Discussion with professional tutor – any questions following their first day in school.

CHECKLIST Induction – subject department/faculty

■ Colleagues

- formally introduce the student teachers to all of your departmental colleagues including laboratory assistants or other ancillary staff attached to the department.

■ Facilities and resources

- show them around the departmental block, explaining the use of any departmental offices, work and preparation areas.

- show them where resources are stored and take them through procedures for the use of such things as class sets of books, photocopier, computers, TV and video.

■ Procedures and routines

- inform them of any important departmental routines and practices; these could range from arrangements for pupils' use of the teaching block to use of coffee/tea-making facilities in the departmental office.

■ Curriculum

- give them a brief introduction to departmental/faculty policy on such matters as grouping of pupils, assessment, recording and reporting

- provide them with schemes of work to help them get a feel of the department's work.

■ Expectations and plans

- go through what you expect of the student teachers in terms of commitment, reliability and enthusiasm. Encourage them to talk about what they are hoping to do and gain from their time in school

- go through a preliminary programme with them and discuss ways in which they will be working with you and your colleagues

- go through the school calendar and pick out events and dates relevant to the student teachers. Be clear about which meetings – full staff, departmental, parental consultation – they are expected to attend.

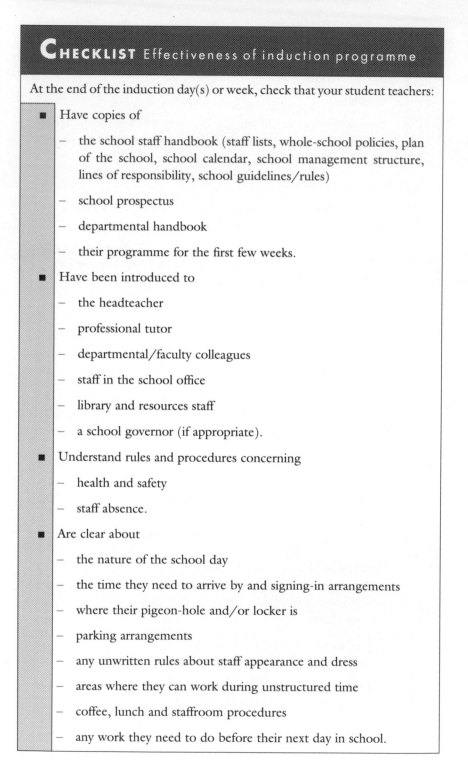

CHECKLIST Effectiveness of induction programme

At the end of the induction day(s) or week, check that your student teachers:

■ Have copies of

– the school staff handbook (staff lists, whole-school policies, plan of the school, school calendar, school management structure, lines of responsibility, school guidelines/rules)

– school prospectus

– departmental handbook

– their programme for the first few weeks.

■ Have been introduced to

– the headteacher

– professional tutor

– departmental/faculty colleagues

– staff in the school office

– library and resources staff

– a school governor (if appropriate).

■ Understand rules and procedures concerning

– health and safety

– staff absence.

■ Are clear about

– the nature of the school day

– the time they need to arrive by and signing-in arrangements

– where their pigeon-hole and/or locker is

– parking arrangements

– any unwritten rules about staff appearance and dress

– areas where they can work during unstructured time

– coffee, lunch and staffroom procedures

– any work they need to do before their next day in school.

Drawing up an effective programme – general points

Monitoring and modifying

However tricky it is to draw up a programme – and, as suggested earlier, you have to take account of a number of interests and needs – it is important that above all it is appropriate to the student teachers' needs as learner teachers. This means monitoring their progress – through talking and working with them, talking with colleagues and with tutors from the university/college in their visits to school – and modifying the programme in the light of their progress and current needs. This is illustrated by the following examples, in which mentors talk about their experience of amending their student teachers' programmes.

EXAMPLE Monitoring and modifying

1. A couple of years ago the student I had was very quick to learn. She took observation seriously, got on well with everyone and was very enthusiastic about becoming a teacher. She was really alert to what was going on in classrooms and she used to ask us very searching questions. I did some collaborative teaching with her with two of my classes, one in Year 7 and the other in Year 9. Within a few weeks it was clear from what I was seeing as well as from what my colleagues were saying about her that I needed to adjust the programme as she was learning so quickly and well. To start with we changed the way we worked together with the two classes – she became the senior partner and I moved more into the background. Then with another teacher she began to take complete lessons so that she took the class twice a week while he took their other three lessons.

2. After Simon had been with us a while and was now spending most of his time in school teaching, I noticed that all was not well with one of the classes he was teaching. A group of four girls was becoming quite disruptive and this really threw him. The class was not working as well as it had been and everything was getting a bit ragged at the edges. We talked about this and decided to change his programme to give him a chance to observe this particular class with a number of other teachers in other subjects.

Selecting classes (and teachers)

During the course of their training, student teachers need to work with pupils across the full range of age and ability. This does not, however, mean that they need to be working with the full range all the time; it is for you to decide what would be appropriate for their learning at any stage in their development. At some time all student teachers need the experience of teaching challenging classes which are not especially well motivated. To give them such a class before they are confident and skilful in terms of classroom management and control would be detrimental to the class as well as to the student teacher. Consideration of pupils' needs is also important when giving the student teachers experience of examination classes in Years 11 and 13. In such cases it makes sense for them to be working in close collaboration with the class teacher. In the same way it is important for the student teachers to see a range of practice and to work with more than one teacher. Yet, to place a student with a teacher who is thoroughly disillusioned with teaching or with someone who believes that training is irrelevant would be counter-productive and very disheartening for someone about to enter the profession.

Remembering they are learners

Unguided practice and unthinking involvement in activities in school is not the most effective way of learning. To make the most of their time in school, student teachers' learning needs to be guided and focused. Moreover, they also need time to think and to make sense of all that they will be learning in school. The amount of teaching they do will, of course, increase as they become more skilful and confident. However, it would be unreasonable if at any time they were teaching more than 60 per cent of the average timetable for a classroom teacher without other responsibilities.

Leaving room for other activities

Since learning about teaching can properly take place outside of the classroom, the programme should leave time for the student teachers to investigate resources, collect material/data for assignments, plan lessons, and find out about whole-school issues. When they are first with you in school, you may wish to adopt a 'directive' approach to the use of this non-contact time to ensure that they are getting as much as possible from their time in school.

Putting in fixed slots

Build into the programme any fixed slots such as the time set aside for you to meet them, or a regular meeting for student teachers (alongside newly qualified teachers perhaps) led by the professional tutor.

Drawing up a programme – early weeks

When they are first in school, the student teachers' programme is likely to vary from week to week as you try to:

- give them a broad picture of the work of your department/faculty

- help them to focus on different aspects of teaching.

Figure 1.1 (overleaf) shows the kind of programme student teachers might have when they have been in school for about three weeks.

Figure 1.1 *Early weeks: a student teacher's programme*

Week's focus: Classroom management (resources and pupil management)
Mentor: CH
Other teachers: LK, RM
Tutor time: Observation this week of a Year 9 group with MD

	MONDAY	TUESDAY	WEDNESDAY	THURSDAY	FRIDAY
8.45	Tutor time	Tutor time	Tutor time	Tutor time	Tutor time
9.00	(Use this time to check on resources for lesson 5)	11A LK Observation focusing on ground rules, sanctions, etc.			7C (CH) Teaching whole class
10.00	8L CH Observation of management strategies	Debriefing with LK – how standards established and maintained *Dept. office*		7C (CH) Teaching whole class	
11.00				(Debriefing)	
11.20	Mentor period to include debriefing from period 2	10A RM Teaching small group	8L CH Supporting individuals	Seminar run by **professional tutor** *Meetings Room*	8N CH Collaborative Teaching – conducting feedback from groupwork
12.20					
1.15	Tutor time	Tutor time	Tutor time	Tutor time	Tutor time
1.20		7C (CH) Teaching (CH acting as learning support)	10A RM Teaching small group		8L CH Supporting individuals
2.20	8N CH Responsible for resources		8N CH Collaborative Teaching – introducing video, setting group tasks	11A LK Observation focusing on introductions, transitions, endings	
3.20		(Debriefing 7C)		(Debriefing 11A)	

Initials in brackets = teacher in classroom but not responsible for lesson.

Whatever their programme, it is important to remember that, with any class, individual responsibilities need to be clear. How are the student teachers working in the classroom? For example: Are they getting to know classes they will be teaching by acting as classroom assistants? Are they engaged in collaborative teaching, involved in the planning, teaching and evaluation of the lesson? If they are working collaboratively, who is responsible for collecting in and marking work?

The more focused the work of the student teachers, the greater is the potential for effective learning. In any lesson, and in whatever way student teachers are working – as passive observer, teacher colleague engaged in collaborative teaching, classroom assistant working with individuals and small groups, teacher of the whole class for a complete lesson – the purpose of the activity in relation to their learning needs to be clear.

Drawing up a programme later – a teaching timetable

CHECKLIST Drawing up a teaching timetable: the process

Teaching timetables for student teachers are likely to emerge after a lengthy consultation process. They will be affected by different departmental and school imperatives, but there may well be a number of stages in common:

- Consult colleagues about suitable groups with which the student teachers can continue working or start afresh. Bear in mind the idiosyncrasies of the school campus – the distances between teaching blocks or school sites.

- Ask the student teachers about their views on the timetable.

- Build in fixed slots such as the mentor period, tutor/form period, seminar with professional tutor.

- Produce a draft timetable that indicates any 'clashes'.

- Consult all interested parties – the student teachers and the class teachers concerned – before coming up with 'compromises'.

- Circulate amended proposals to all interested parties including the professional tutor and, in schemes where the partnership is close, the tutor from the university/college.

- Produce the final timetable with a key that indicates when the student teacher is working alone with the class and where collaborative teaching is happening.

- Circulate the timetable.

- Be prepared to modify it in the light of experience.

Figure 1.2   *Later: a student teacher's timetable*

Mentor: CH
Other teachers: LK, RM
Form tutor: HY

	MONDAY	TUESDAY	WEDNESDAY	THURSDAY	FRIDAY
8.45 – 9.00	Tutor time (HY)	Tutor time (HY)	Tutor time (HY)	Tutor time (HY)	Tutor time (HY)
9.00 – 10.00	12C1 (CH)	11A LK Collaborative Teaching	7B (CH)		
10.00 – 11.00	8L CH Mentor teaching – student teacher observing	12C1 (CH)		9R (RM)	11A (LK) Collaborative Teaching
11.00 – 11.20					
11.20 – 12.20	**Mentor period**		8L CH Mentor teaching – student teacher observing	**Seminar run by professional tutor**	**7B CH**
12.20 – 1.15					
1.15 – 1.20	Tutor time (HY)	Tutor time (HY)	Tutor time (HY)	Tutor time (HY)	Tutor time (HY)
1.20 – 2.20		9R (RM)	12C1 (CH)	7B (CH)	8L CH
2.20 –	9R (RM)			11A LK Collaborative Teaching	

Initials in brackets = teacher in classroom but not responsible for lesson.

It is useful for student teachers to be doing some observation at this time, perhaps one or two periods a week. As their own practice develops, they can 'see' more in other classrooms; it is as if they now have a better understanding of what they don't know, yet need to know. Many also are interested in seeing teachers in other subject areas working with the pupils they themselves are teaching. Figure 1.2 is an example of a timetable for student teachers nearing the end of their course. Although at this later stage your student teacher(s)' programme will be presented much more obviously as a teaching timetable, this does not mean that they will be acting as the sole class teacher for each of these groups every lesson. Their programme each week still needs to take account of their needs as learners and of the needs of your pupils. For example, with the Year 11 class in Figure 1.2 about to sit their GCSEs, the student teacher is working alongside the regular class teacher – working with small groups who want to revise particular topics, giving help to individual pupils and in one lesson exploiting the fact that there are two teachers to present a revision exercise as a debate in role.

Having taken sole responsibility for some classes for a number of weeks (with the class teacher observing regularly), the student teachers may have identified particular aspects that they would like to explore further by watching an experienced teacher again, now that they know what to look for. So, in the week shown in Figure 1.2 the student teacher has asked his mentor to teach a complete lesson with 8L so that he can see how the mentor caters for the wide range of ability in the group and how particular pupils respond to different types of activity.

Ensuring the timetable is suitable for the individual student teacher

CHECKLIST

- Are the classes they are working with appropriate?

- Are they continuing to work collaboratively in some lessons?

- Are they working with you for sufficient time to enable you to guide their development and monitor their progress?

- Are the teachers with whose classes they are working clear about their own responsibilities, not only to the pupils but to the student teachers?

- Are these teachers clear about diagnostic assessment (Unit 3) and, when appropriate, partnership supervision (Unit 7)?

- Is their workload manageable and appropriate?

  - how many different classes are they working with?

  - how much marking are they doing?

  - does the timetable allow them to get from one class to another in time?

  - are they having to prepare a lot of material from scratch or are there detailed schemes of work they can make use of and adapt?

  - have they got some non-contact time every day?

- Is there a need to modify the timetable? For example, would it be useful for a confident and skilful student to take on a new class that she or he has not worked with before?

SUMMARY

School placements provide student teachers not only with the opportunity to practise teaching but also to learn from the expertise of experienced teachers – you as their mentor, and your colleagues. However, if student teachers are to make effective use of this opportunity their learning needs to be carefully managed. You need to provide your student teachers with a programme for their time in school that offers them protection in the early stages of their training and develops as they become more competent as classroom teachers. In devising a programme that meets their needs as learners you also have to consider the best interests of your pupils and of your colleagues. To do it well you need to:

- *plan carefully even before the student teachers arrive*

- *recognize the student teachers' position as adult learners*

- *liaise closely with your colleagues and support them in their work with the student teachers*

- *be prepared to modify the student teachers' programme in the light of experience, and as their teaching develops*

- *be realistic in your expectations of the student teachers, your colleagues and yourself!*

Observation

It is common practice for student teachers to observe what happens in experienced teachers' classrooms. For that observation to be useful it needs to have a clear purpose and be conducted in a way that is appropriate for that purpose. There are different kinds of observation which can be useful and you can help guide your student teachers in understanding and appreciating what each can offer them. Focused and purposeful observation can be very fruitful. Unfocused observation, without a clear purpose, is generally demoralizing and counter-productive.

WHY DO IT?

The need for guided observation

Observation is a well-established element in what student teachers are generally asked to do in schools. It has been normal practice since teacher training began for student teachers to observe experienced teachers and their pupils at work, especially in the early stages of school practice before they start teaching themselves; but too often this observation has not been useful.

Anyone learning a complex skill finds it helpful to observe highly skilled performances which can provide 'models', before going on to practise the skill. The need to observe other people first applies to teaching and to the many complex skills it involves. For many student teachers, however, observation turns out to be unhelpful, and it is not unusual for them impatiently to dismiss it as a waste of time. The reasons for this include:

- Experienced teachers' teaching is often so fluent that it looks easy: the skill, which cannot be seen by the observer, is very largely in the expert information-processing and decision-making that is going on.

- Student teachers only see what they already understand, and when they are first in schools they do not know enough to see how complex teaching is.

40

- Student teachers have already spent thousands of hours in classrooms as pupils. At first, still with this pupil perspective, everything in classrooms looks familiar and obvious, and they can find it difficult to see things in the way that teachers do.

- Student teachers often have strong preconceptions about what kinds of teachers they want to be. They are quick to judge the teachers they observe as falling short of these preconceptions and therefore think they have little to learn from them.

- Student teachers are generally keen to prove themselves as teachers. They are eager to get on with teaching and to learn from their own practice rather than from observing others.

Given these obstacles, for observation to be useful it must be directed towards a clear purpose. Student teachers need guidance both about the purpose of any particular observation and about how to observe effectively.

EXAMPLE Making observation work

A mentor with many years' experience supervising students on teaching practice explains how she now sets up observation for her student teachers: 'In the old days I used to make my students sit at the back of lessons and make notes, and they used to do this for the first couple of weeks of their time in school. I suppose I did this because that's what I'd done when I was trained. Anyway, they didn't seem to learn much from it and they found it very boring (I managed to get this out of one of them when he'd finished his course). Now I make sure that the observation is much more focused and that we're all clear why they're observing a particular lesson. I also make sure that they don't go from a diet of undiluted observation to no observation at all. They have an observation slot every week even when they're in full flight in their own teaching'.

Traditionally, student teachers observed lessons sitting at the back of classrooms taking copious notes. It is not always necessary to observe lessons in this passive way. Student teachers can learn as much, or more, from observation when they are active in the classroom while, for example, acting as a classroom assistant, engaging in collaborative teaching, or joining a group of pupils. The most effective way of observing any lesson will depend on the purpose and focus of the particular observation.

Ways in which observation can be useful

Focused observation can serve a number of different purposes. Through guided observation student teachers can:

- **Be helped to shift from a pupil to a teacher perspective**
  They need to get a realistic awareness of what pupils do and can do, and at the same time learn to see classrooms from the perspective of a teacher.

- **Learn to analyse what is happening in classrooms**
  Student teachers, unused to detailed analysis of what is happening in lessons, tend to see things in very broad terms. They will obviously recognize that a particular lesson has involved teacher exposition, question and answer, and pupil work in small groups, for example. They are, however, unlikely to appreciate that during the question and answer session the teacher used a variety of questioning techniques, or that different demands were made of different pupils as they began their group work. Focused observation requires student teachers to analyse what is happening – to make distinctions between open and closed questions, for example, or to record the different type of attention that pupils receive from the teacher (disciplinary, support, opportunity to perform, etc.). This kind of analysis can help equip them with new ways of thinking about teaching. By observing teachers in this way they can begin to understand the kind of fine distinctions that they will need to apply in analysing and refining their own teaching.

- **Get a sense of the standards which teachers set**
  Through observing different teachers with different classes, student teachers can see what the teachers in a school find appropriate and acceptable in the way of pupils' behaviour – noise levels, movement, punctuality, concentration and effort. They can also see how the standard and amount of work teachers expect from pupils are affected by the age and ability of the class.

- **Discover different ways of doing things**
  Through observation of different teachers, student teachers can learn different ways of doing those things that have to be done by all teachers – beginning and ending lessons, setting tasks, setting up groupwork.

- **Learn to monitor the progress of a lesson**
  Student teachers often find pacing and timing in lessons very difficult. Observation of a lesson, focusing on the length and variety of activities, and the amount of time pupils spend on given tasks, can

help them to understand how a lesson progresses. Knowledge of the teacher's plans can also help them to see how a teacher responds to developments and adapts plans in the light of pupil response. The benefits of this kind of observation, when the student teacher has a knowledge and understanding of the plans for the lesson, are discussed more fully in Unit 4 – Collaborative Teaching.

■ **Identify things which they do not understand, and which can provide a basis for discussion with the teacher after the lesson**
Often with observation, observers supply their own answers to any questions which crop up, and that can be misleading. Student teachers need to recognize that teachers have their own rationale for what they are doing. To uncover what the teacher was thinking they need to ask questions, such as: 'How did the teacher get that group at the back to work so hard?' and 'What made her use a game to introduce that topic?' Instead of supplying their own answers to such questions, they need to talk with the teacher after the lesson to find out what was in his or her mind. This type of observation is so important that a complete unit – Unit 5 – Opening Up Your Practice – has been given over to it.

GUIDELINES FOR THE DIFFERENT KINDS OF OBSERVATION

From pupil to teacher perspective

When to do it
When they first go into schools all student teachers need to get a sense of the reality of teaching from the perspective of a *teacher*. They need to face up to the situations that face *teachers* rather than those that face pupils before they can *begin* to learn how to teach in classrooms.

What you can hope to achieve
Many student teachers begin their training course assuming that subject knowledge, enthusiasm, friendliness and commitment are all they will need. This kind of observation in the early stages can help them to realize how much they will have to learn.

Selection of classes to be observed
In the first few weeks they need to observe you and your colleagues with classes which you find difficult as well as others which are easier. It is with the difficult classes that your expertise is likely to be most apparent, and in observing you student teachers will be able to see that nothing can be taken for granted. A

classroom atmosphere conducive to learning, pupils' concentration, motivation and understanding come from effective teaching.

Preparation

The main guidance to give them is that in their observation they should identify with the teacher, imagining themselves in the teacher's shoes, facing up to the situations which confront the teacher and deciding how to deal with these. They should consider questions such as:

- What are the things that I would find most difficult if I were the teacher in this situation?

- Would I want to deal with them in the same way as the teacher is doing?

- If so, would I be able to?

- If not, what alternative course of action would I prefer?

- Would I be able to do that?

- If I did that, what would the probable consequences be?

Follow-up

Discussion with the student teacher after the lesson should help you to find out how realistic they are about the problems teachers face, and their ability to handle them. If, after a number of observations, it is clear that the student teachers are underestimating the difficulty of some particular aspect of teaching – such as classroom management, clear explanations, whole-class question and answer – it would be useful to get them to focus on that aspect in future observations. Continued lack of realism which shows itself in overconfidence may have to be dealt with by giving them some limited experience of responsibility for one of the more challenging classes they observed.

This approach to observation can be used at any stage of their training when helping student teachers to face up to aspects of their own teaching that they are neglecting. It can be easier for them to start facing up to something they have ignored, such as catering for pupils with writing difficulties or giving too much attention to extrovert pupils at the expense of the quieter ones, by first focusing on the same aspect when observing an experienced and skilful teacher.

Possible problems

Student teachers will not overnight abandon their preconceptions about teaching – including the belief that they already know the answers. On the other hand, they are unlikely to reveal such arrogant thinking to you; they generally realize what you and your colleagues expect of them and what attitudes you are looking for. You may well need a lot of patience as you work to build up a relationship with them that enables both of you to go beyond politeness, while at the same time persuading them to face up to the realities of teaching.

Learning to analyse what is happening in classrooms

When to do it

This kind of observation is useful at any stage in a student teacher's training or qualified teacher's career. It is especially helpful when learning new skills or strategies as it is concerned with learning to use new concepts in thinking about what goes on in classrooms.

What you can hope to achieve

By analysing in detail particular aspects of classroom teaching and learning, student teachers learn to use new concepts in thinking about classroom events and activities. After practice in applying these distinctions to other people's teaching they are more able to apply them to their own practice.

> ## EXAMPLE Learning to make distinctions
>
> *The comments that follow illustrate how successful this approach can be: 'From the start Stuart (the student teacher) was at ease with the pupils. Some of the students I've worked with have taken quite a while to learn how to talk to individual 14-year-olds, to be at ease with them, but he was at home from the beginning. So, when he was teaching he had no problems interacting with the pupils, but I felt that a lot of time was being wasted in his lessons and that a lot of the teacher/pupil chat going on wasn't necessarily helpful. To get him to understand that it was important to differentiate between different kinds of contact with the pupils, he observed a colleague's lesson with an observation schedule based on teacher/pupil contact. As a result of this he looked at his own teaching in a different sort of way. He realized that most of the time he spent talking with the pupils had little or nothing to do with the work they were doing, and that he was hardly spending any time at all in his lessons helping individuals to understand the work'.*

Deciding what to observe

This kind of observation is useful when there are distinctions that you want to bring to the attention of your student teacher. Only you can determine what aspects of classroom activity are worth concentrating on in the light of your student teacher's understanding and learning. The following are simply examples of the kinds of things you might focus on, and the possible categories within each focus:

- types of teacher contact with individual pupils

  - gender of the pupil concerned
  and whether the contact is initiated by teacher or pupil
  and what the communication is about – lesson content, discipline, classroom management, etc.

- how different pupils spend their time in a lesson

  - whether or not they appear to be 'on task'
  and who or what they are interacting with/paying attention to: teacher, other pupils, their own concerns, other sources.

- teachers' questions in classroom discussion

  - closed: obviously having correct answers

  - apparently open: but, as can be seen by the teacher's response to answers, having hidden 'correct' answers

  - genuinely open questions.

- classroom talk
  Teachers' and pupils' talk may be categorized according to its cognitive level as:

  - assertions of fact

  - expressions of opinion and value-judgements

  - interpretations of meaning

  - explanations and justifications.

Preparation

For student teachers to see any value in this kind of observation, they need to:

- recognize the importance of the concept underlying the observation (it is likely, therefore, to emerge from discussion of their teaching)

- realize that they are practising making the distinctions in order to apply them to their own teaching.

Before the observation it is worth going through the categories to make sure that the student teacher fully understands the distinctions being made and how to recognize them in the classroom. It is also important to be clear about practical procedures:

- Is the observation schedule/system relevant to the whole lesson?

- Exactly which aspects of the lesson are to be categorized?

- If time-sampling is to be used, what frequency of recording will the student teacher be able to manage?

- If the focus is on what pupils do, how many pupils are to be observed? How are they to be chosen? What procedure will be used for recording each of their activities?

Follow-up

Observation of this kind produces quantitative evidence about the relative frequency of different kinds of events and activities in classrooms. It is important for the student teacher and the observed teacher to discuss the evidence. The teacher will want to comment on what the record shows, whether or not they are satisfied with such a pattern of events, and why. The discussion also gives the student teacher an opportunity to raise issues of interest to them, perhaps explaining the implications of what they have seen for their own teaching. The student teacher, having tried out using the concept in observing someone else's teaching, is then able to put it into operation in planning, teaching and, probably with your help, in monitoring his or her own practice.

Getting a sense of the standards which teachers set

When to do it

Observation for this purpose should in general come fairly early on in the student teachers' time in school. As they face up to successive aspects of teaching and find appropriate ways of thinking about each aspect, so they will need to find out what standards can reasonably be set for each.

What you can hope to achieve

Naturally, teachers vary in the strictness and the nature of the standards they set for all the different aspects of classroom teaching: indeed, any individual teacher's standards may well vary from class to class. The recollections of a head of department emphasize this point:

> In my department, not only do we all work in different ways, but each one of us changes things depending on the class. For example, I know I'm not consistent in the rule I apply about putting hands up to answer questions. It's something I insist on with Year 7 at the start of the year, but at the same time I tolerate Year 11 calling out. It's because the GCSE group know what's acceptable and I can trust them to volunteer ideas without it degenerating into chaos. Year 7 aren't able to judge what's appropriate and regulate their behaviour so I have to set clear standards and stick to them. Although the rules seem to be different, nobody would accept shouting out or shouting each other down. With all our classes we all insist that pupils listen to each other.

The great majority of experienced teachers do seem to share a sense of what is generally acceptable. Through observation student teachers can acquire a sense of the range of acceptable standards.

Preparation

Usually you will not need to set this up as a specific kind of observation. As long as the student teachers are having some experience of observation for other purposes in a variety of classrooms, they can pick up a sense of appropriate standards. It is only when they are having problems in the classroom because they are setting standards which are too lenient or too strict that you may want to guide them in focused observation for this purpose. In these circumstances it would be helpful for them to observe a number of teachers and classes focusing their observation on the identified problem area.

If the problem is that the student teacher is taking too much or too little account of differences among classes in age or ability, then it would be useful to select a range of classes that show how you and your colleagues adjust your standards when working with different classes.

Follow-up

You can help your student teachers to reflect on:

- variations and commonalities across teachers and across age and ability groups

- ways in which their own practice falls outside the normal range.

Your student teachers may find it difficult to accept that the standards they wish to set or are setting are simply not appropriate for the class. It can be difficult to persuade student teachers that the standards they are setting are inappropriate. It may be easier for them to accept that the pupils are used to certain standards and find it difficult to adapt to different ones; and you may be able to use that argument to persuade your student teachers to modify their standards.

Discovering different ways of doing things

When to do it

Observation for this purpose is useful at any time. Whatever aspect of teaching they are concentrating on, student teachers need first to learn – almost certainly through observation – one way of doing it that they can try for themselves. At every stage, however, they should be encouraged to look for additional ways of doing things which they can add to their repertoires.

What you can hope to achieve

Student teachers need to develop an extensive range of teaching strategies and varied repertoires for managing different kinds of classroom activity – for example, explaining things effectively; facilitating practical work; setting up and running group discussions, role-plays, simulations and investigations and the whole range of teaching strategies they should be learning to use. They need to recognize that some ways will suit them better than others and, more importantly, that some ways will be more suitable than others for different classes and for different circumstances.

Preparation

As with all observation, make sure that your student teachers are clear why they are observing a lesson and what the focus is. If possible, match the particular skill or aspect of teaching the student teacher is concentrating on with teachers who are especially skilful in that area.

Observation of this kind will be most effective if the teacher to be observed can spend a few minutes beforehand with the student teacher explaining what the key aspects of the intended approach will be and, when appropriate, which parts of the lesson it would be most useful to concentrate on.

Follow-up

A few minutes talking with the observed teacher immediately after the lesson (perhaps on the way to the next lesson), highlighting the things done and discussing the appropriateness of the approach for the class and the circumstances can help the student teacher to make the transition from seeing to understanding. Encourage the student teachers to try out the same approach in their own teaching (with an appropriate class) as soon as possible after the observation.

Figure 2.1 *Observation: summary*

Purpose of observation	Most appropriate time
Shifting from a pupil to a teacher perspective *Helping student teachers to be realistic about the demands of teaching and their ability to handle them*	■ at the beginning, for them to see what teaching entails ■ at any time when you feel they are neglecting important aspects of teaching
Learning to analyse what is happening in classrooms *Enabling student teachers to recognize that while variations properly exist between the rules and expectations of different teachers, these fall within certain acceptable bounds*	■ early on ■ at any time if the standards they are setting in their own teaching are inappropriate
Discovering different ways of doing things *Encouraging student teachers to appreciate that teachers can bring about pupil learning in a variety of ways and to extend their own repertoires of skills and strategies*	■ at any time
Learning to monitor the progress of a lesson *Bringing home to student teachers the importance of pacing and timing and the need for flexibility*	■ early on when you are providing them with a protected environment in which to begin teaching ■ later, focusing on the need for flexibility and how teachers adapt their plans
Identifying things which student teachers do not understand, which can provide a basis for discussion with the teacher after the lesson *Taking student teachers beyond what can be observed and giving them access to the teachers' thinking and decision-making*	■ most useful in the second half of their training

Summary

Observation forms an essential part of any student teacher's experience in schools. However, unless their observation is guided and has a clear purpose the opportunities for learning that it presents are generally wasted. It is natural for student teachers to observe lessons at the beginning of their time in schools, but guided observation has a valuable part to play throughout their training. The different purposes of observation are summarized in Figure 2.1.

ASSESSMENT AND SUPERVISION

Student teachers need regular assessment of, and feedback on, their teaching. Assessment and supervision is when the mentor assesses the competence of a student teacher as a classroom teacher and, as a result, offers strategies to improve and develop his or her knowledge and skills. It occurs when the student teacher teaches and the mentor observes the teaching. Following this the mentor and student teacher discuss the observed teaching. As a result of this discussion, targets are set for the student teacher.

The number of times the mentor does this will obviously depend on the individual student teacher's needs at any given time. When student teachers are in school full-time it is reasonable to expect that *every* teacher working with them will observe at least one lesson per class each week, whatever the student teacher's level of competence.

LOOKING FOR COMPETENCE

All student teachers, whatever their subject, background, preferred ways of working and personal characteristics, need to be able to attain the competences expected of newly qualified teachers. The competences in the DFE's (1992) list are expressed in broad terms. This list provides a starting point in defining what can be expected of beginning teachers. In many partnership schemes between schools and universities/colleges these competences are broken down into more manageable components. Such an agreed list provides the student teachers with a set of criteria which they can use to:

- analyse their teaching, with the help of their mentor and others

- set goals for themselves and note their progress

- identify areas of weakness on which they need to concentrate.

A list of this kind also provides you with a framework within which to undertake assessment and supervision.

All teachers need to be able to 'maintain pupils' interest and motivation' (DFE, 1992 'competences expected of newly qualified teachers', 2.4.4. Circular 9/92, London: DFE.) for example, and *all* student teachers need to learn how to do that. There is, however, no single 'correct' way of maintaining pupils' interest and motivation. Not only do different teachers bring that about in different ways, but every experienced teacher is likely to have a number of ways of achieving that effect. No two lessons are the same; everything – from the kind of learning one wants to take place, to the state of the weather – can affect what the teacher does. The experienced teacher, therefore, will go about motivating the pupils in a way that suits the circumstances of a particular lesson. Student teachers, with your help, need to learn not only how to achieve these effects, but also gradually to build up a repertoire of different ways of achieving these effects in different circumstances.

THE PROCESS

Assessment and supervision is a cyclical process as illustrated by Figure 3.1. It includes:

- discussion with the student teacher before the lesson

- observation of the student teacher

- discussion following the observed lesson in which targets are set. These targets are likely to provide the focus for the next cycle.

Your task as mentor in managing the student teachers' learning in relation to classroom teaching can be greatly helped if all the teachers working with your

Figure 3.1 *The process of assessment and supervision*

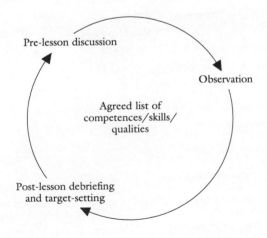

student teachers use a proforma both to guide and record the whole process of assessment. (See, for example, Figure 3.2.)

Pre-lesson discussion

Discussion before the lesson is needed to maximize the effectiveness of your observation and the student teachers' learning related to it. The length and nature of the discussion will depend on a number of factors such as:

- time available

- the student teacher's needs

- how much time has passed since the student teacher was last observed.

During the pre-lesson discussion it is important to do the following.

- *Establish the focus of observation* – it is necessary to take account of the student teacher's overall progress and level of confidence. In the first few weeks in school, for example, they tend to be consumed with concerns of discipline and control. It would, therefore, be unproductive to focus on other issues to the exclusion of their concerns.

- *Go through the plans for the lesson* – in the early days the lesson may well have been jointly planned by you and the student teachers: in the pre-lesson discussion therefore, you will merely be checking that they are fully prepared for the lesson. Later, as the student teacher(s) take responsibility for the planning of the lesson, they will need to take you through the plans, outlining aims and how they are to be achieved.

- *Sort out the timing of the post-lesson debriefing* – the post-lesson debriefing should be carried out as soon after the observed lesson as is reasonably possible. Student teachers are always anxious to find out what their mentor thinks of the lesson. Moreover, so much happens in an 'ordinary' school day that the details of the lesson could become blurred in your mind. It is worth considering choosing a lesson because it is followed by a 'free' period, break, or lunch time, to guarantee time for debriefing.

- *Decide on how the observation is to be carried out* – when deciding *how* to observe a lesson it is worth considering:

    - the agreed focus

    - the type of lesson

    - the student teacher's level of confidence, self-awareness

    - needs of the pupils

If, for example, you are observing the lesson to see if pupils understand what the work is about, it would make sense – at some time during the lesson – to act as the student teacher's assistant and to work with pupils, rather than sit at the back of the class making copious notes. Within a single lesson, it may be appropriate to move from one way of observing to another, as the phases of the lesson unfold.

If you are using a proforma similar to the one in Figure 3.2, the sections on 'Agreed focus' and 'Agreed method of observation' can be filled in during the pre-lesson discussion, as illustrated in Figure 3.2.

Observation

Part of the lesson or all of it?

To get a clear idea of how the student teacher is progressing, it is important to observe whole lessons rather than simply 'popping in to see how they're getting on'. There are, however, occasions when it would be valid to observe a part of the lesson because of the chosen focus.

EXAMPLE The focus determines the mode of observation

An English student teacher and her mentor had decided that the focus for the mentor's observation would be 'endings'. The student teacher had been teaching on a number of occasions and her mentor was generally happy with the way she was developing as a classroom teacher, but lessons always seemed to end in a rush. The mentor was concerned not only with these messy endings, but also with the fact that the student teacher's perception of her teaching was coloured by the endings; she tended to be dismissive of the whole lesson because of the messiness of the final five minutes or so.

The mentor, through previous observation, realized that the problem occurred in those lessons in which homework was to be set; quite simply, the student teacher was only allowing three minutes for an explanation of the homework with no time for questions, clarification, etc.

The mentor worked with the student teacher to plan the next lesson, paying particular attention to timing and pacing. This time, the mentor taught and the student teacher observed. The student teacher noticed that the mentor allowed more than 10 minutes for the setting of homework – pupils writing it down, questions from pupils, homework deadline set, etc.

During the subsequent lesson the roles were reversed, with the mentor observing the last 20 minutes of the lesson to see if the student teacher could put into practice what she had observed.

Figure 3.2 *Example of a completed proforma*

Classroom Observation and Debriefing	
Student Teacher: Pete **Class:** 10L **Date:** 30th Nov	

Agreed focus:	Agreed method of observation:	
Lesson ending – giving out homework and packing away.	Assisting individuals during main part of lesson. Lesson ending; noting instructions & observing pupil actions	These sections are completed during the pre-lesson discussion.

Notes relating to focus

Strengths displayed by student teacher	Strategies/techniques recommended	
Clear instructions – that they were to write down homework. Use of board as reinforcement. Good timing – enough time given for both recording homework and packing away.	Ensure pupils who can't find homework diary are told to write homework down elsewhere (back of book?) Don't allow anyone to go until everyone is standing quietly.	Aide-mémoire for mentor. Key points from observation ready for debriefing discussion.

Aide-mémoire for mentor. Recommended strategies that come to mind. |

Other points for discussion

• The use of video – the need to have it cued to the right place before the lesson. • What strategies can you think of to deal with latecomers? • What are quick & effective ways of distributing resources.	Other issues which have arisen in the lesson which need discussion.

Action	
1. Try out making everyone stand quietly before they can leave at end of lesson (all groups). 2. Explain procedures for recording homework – ie in homework diary or back of book. 3. Ask latecomers simply to sit down quietly & then see them at the end. 4. Ask a pupil to give out the resources. 5. Make sure the video is cued for tomorrow's year 10 group (check at break).	Should include suggested teaching group, period, etc.

Sometimes you may want to teach the class for part of the lesson, observing the student teacher teaching for the remainder of the lesson.

Collecting information

Depending on the agreed focus, different sorts of information will be useful to you in analysing the student teacher's competence. If, for example, the focus is on explanation, it may be useful to record verbatim the words used by the student teacher in explaining new terms or concepts to the class. If the focus is on classroom control it may be worth noting the student teacher's use of non-verbal signals as well as the language used to reprimand pupils and examples of pupil behaviour (or misbehaviour).

Pointers to successful debriefing

Time and place

To be most useful the debriefing needs to take place:

- as soon as possible after the observed lesson and preferably within 24 hours

- away from other people and possible interruptions.

Listening

It is very important to give the student teachers an opportunity to talk about the lesson. By finding out something about how they are feeling and how they saw the lesson, you can decide what they are capable of understanding and learning at that particular time. The comments of an experienced maths mentor underline the importance of listening:

> It's very important to listen to them. That's a skill mentors need, listening skills, and they don't necessarily have them. Although mentors have got a lot of information to get over, they've got to learn to be quiet at times as well and let the student teacher talk. Unless you know what's going on in their head, how they saw the lesson and so on, you can't know how to help them.

It is helpful, therefore, to start the debriefing with a general open question such as:

- What did you think of the lesson?

- How do you feel it went?

- What do you think went well?

EXAMPLE Deciding how to proceed in the light of the student teachers' comments

1. On being asked how she thought the lesson had gone, a maths student teacher said 'chaotic'. The mentor, feeling that the student teacher tended to be pessimistic and too self-critical, thought it important to begin by looking at what he saw as the student teacher's achievements in the lesson.

2. An English student teacher's response to being asked what had gone well was, 'Nothing – it was disastrous!' The mentor felt that the student teacher's perception of the lesson had been coloured by its ending – the agreed focus of observation – which was indeed disorganized and muddled. The mentor therefore began by focusing on those aspects of the lesson that had gone well before examining the ending to the lesson and offering various strategies for the student teacher to consider.

3. A history mentor, concerned that her student teacher had been rather vague about his aims for the lesson at the planning stages, began the debriefing by asking him how he thought the lesson had gone. His reply: 'I think most of them understood what they were supposed to be doing, and got on with it ok', brought home to her the differences between the student teacher's and her own perceptions of the lesson. She decided to ask the student teacher direct, clearly focused questions to enable him to see for himself some of the problems which she had so clearly observed in the lesson: 'What did you set out to achieve in that lesson? What was actually the aim of that lesson in your mind?' As the student teacher tried to explain his aims, he began to see that he hadn't been very clear in his own thinking in preparing the lesson.

Being positive

Student teachers can very easily feel battered and bruised. For many of them, learning to teach is very demanding and frustrating and is quite different from any other kind of learning they've done in the past. The comments of an experienced mentor highlight the importance of emphasizing the positive and building on strengths:

> You always have to find a strength in every lesson because morale is so important. If once they lose their self-confidence, nerves come into play to such an extent that they just can't get over it and they become so nervous in the classroom that they're paralysed. So, identifying strengths is very important.

Breaking it down

Student teachers need help in breaking down teaching into its component parts. They tend to make blanket judgements about their teaching. Thus lessons are 'brilliant', or 'chaotic', or 'disastrous', or 'awful'. As an experienced maths mentor commented,

> Student teachers are often in a hurry. If the lesson's gone well, they're relieved and don't want to examine it; if it's gone badly, they're embarrassed and don't want to dwell on it.

A critical part of your task as mentor is to help the student teacher adopt a more analytical approach to classroom teaching, to move away from sweeping judgements about whole lessons and to focus on particular skills.

EXAMPLE Helping the student teacher to analyse teaching

The focus of the observation in an English lesson had been the student teacher's reading of a story to the class with a follow-up question and answer session. Mentor and student teacher were in agreement that it had gone well, especially in comparison with a similar lesson two weeks earlier. The student teacher was unable to identify why that part of the lesson had gone well, insisting that it had 'just happened'. For those skills to become part of the student teacher's repertoire it was important that she was able to identify them. The mentor therefore explained to the student teacher that she had:

- *read to the class in a clear voice*

- *varied her voice to make the story interesting*

- *scanned the class while reading*

- *asked questions of different kinds at a level the pupils could understand*

- *responded to pupil responses in ways that deepened their understanding of the story*

- *looked positive and enthusiastic.*

It had not simply 'just happened'. That part of the lesson had worked because of the many things the student teacher had done.

Following a broad set pattern

It is useful to structure discussion in the way shown in Figure 3.3.

Shaping the debriefing session in this way helps to:

- ensure some kind of balance

- give priority to the student teacher's perceptions

- underline the positive

- get future discussions going as student teachers learn to use the pattern.

Jointly agreed summary

A summary of the main points arising from the debriefing is useful both for you and the student teacher. Since the whole process of diagnostic assessment and supervision is cyclical, it is probable that the points included in the summary will become part of the focus of the next lesson. If you decide to use a proforma (see Figure 3.2), then it is most useful for the student teacher to keep the completed form in his or her file (professional log), and for you to make a note of the agreed debriefing summary for reference.

COLLEAGUES WORKING WITH STUDENT TEACHERS

It is likely that you as mentor will not be the only teacher to observe the student teacher teach and give them feedback on the observed teaching. Part of your role therefore, is to prepare colleagues for observation and debriefing and, in order to have an overview of the student teacher's progress, to collate colleagues' judgements, assessments and advice. You may find it useful to:

- get departmental or faculty colleagues to use a proforma

- give colleagues a copy of the agreed list of competences, skills and qualities

- discuss and agree on how best to communicate with each other about the student teacher's progress

- use some departmental time to discuss the process of assessment and supervision. (Figure 3.4, which highlights some common myths that may need to be dispelled, can prove a useful basis for discussion.)

Figure 3.3 *Shaping the debriefing*

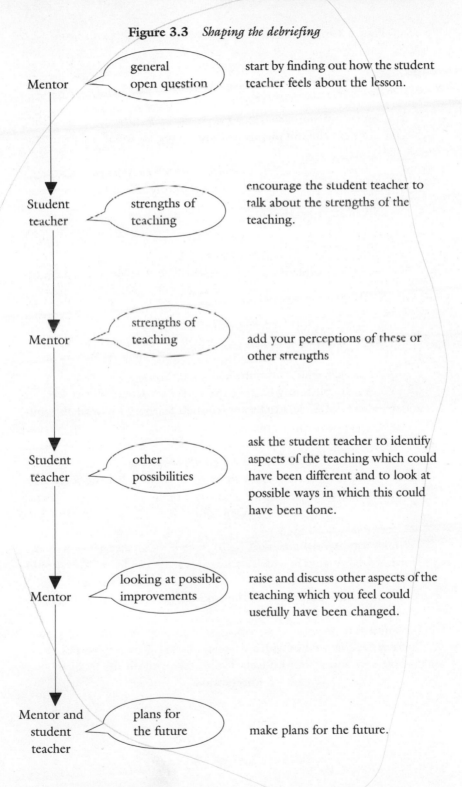

Mentor — general open question — start by finding out how the student teacher feels about the lesson.

Student teacher — strengths of teaching — encourage the student teacher to talk about the strengths of the teaching.

Mentor — strengths of teaching — add your perceptions of these or other strengths

Student teacher — other possibilities — ask the student teacher to identify aspects of the teaching which could have been different and to look at possible ways in which this could have been done.

Mentor — looking at possible improvements — raise and discuss other aspects of the teaching which you feel could usefully have been changed.

Mentor and student teacher — plans for the future — make plans for the future.

Figure 3.4 *Assessment and supervision: challenging the myths*

You can tell how a student teacher is getting on by listening at the door.
You can't get the full picture without being aware of the context.

It is impossible to help a student teacher who is competent.
No matter how good a student teacher is, there is always room for improvement.

If a student teacher hasn't seen what is wrong with a lesson, there is nothing you can do to help.
Your role is to enable the student teachers to develop as teachers by balancing security and challenge.

Good teachers are born, not made.
Your role is to broaden the student teacher's repertoire.

It doesn't matter how often the student teacher is observed.
You must constantly balance the student teachers' desire for independence with the need to move their learning forward through observation and debriefing.

Teachers should always appear experts.
Everyone has experienced difficulties at some time. It is important to be honest with student teachers and to let them know that you are no exception.

The only way to learn is to stand up in front of a class and get on with it.
There are many ways in which a student teacher can learn. You should be aware of the range of possibilities and take care to match the student teachers' experience to the appropriate stage in their learning.

The only way to observe a lesson is to sit at the back of the class writing notes.
There are many ways in which you can observe. The way you can best observe and collect information will depend on the focus of observation.

Summary

Diagnostic assessment and supervision is the critical process by which you:

■ *analyse the classroom teaching of your student teachers*

■ *assess their competence*

■ *develop strategies to help them improve their teaching.*

Judgements about competence must be related to an agreed list of criteria – the competences expected of newly qualified teachers (as defined by the DFE, or an elaboration of these competences developed by your partnership scheme).

Diagnostic assessment and supervision is a cyclical process involving:

■ *pre-lesson discussion*

■ *observation*

■ *debriefing.*

To do it well you need to:

■ *support the student teachers*

   – *by listening to their views*

   – *by underlining their positive achievements*

■ *help the student teachers to analyse their own teaching*

   – *by asking specific questions to focus their thinking*

   – *by discussing in detail what you observed*

■ *help the student teachers to improve their classroom competence*

   – *by suggesting (or developing from their suggestions) strategies for future use*

   – *by setting specific targets.*

COLLABORATIVE TEACHING

Collaborative teaching here is taken to mean any lesson that has been jointly planned and taught by a mentor (or experienced teacher) and student teacher(s). The degree of collaboration involved in the planning may vary considerably. The mentor may well plan the lesson outline and then suggest a specific slot within it for which they would like the student teacher(s) to take responsibility; or, at the other end of the spectrum, both mentor and student teacher(s) may together plan the whole lesson 'from scratch'. Whatever the degree of collaboration, the lesson should be planned to ensure that the student teacher(s) have a *clearly defined responsibility* within it, which is deliberately targeted to help their learning.

WHY DO IT?

The benefits for student teachers' learning

Collaborative teaching can prove a highly effective means of helping student teachers to develop various kinds of new skills or understandings. Collaborative teaching makes two kinds of learning possible:

- *Planning* – learning to plan lessons carefully through being involved in joint planning with you, finding out what you take account of, and identifying with the planning and its consequences.

- *Classroom teaching skills* – learning certain skills through having responsibility for a specified component of the lesson while at the same time identifying with the whole lesson and recognizing the relationship of the part to the whole.

A third kind of learning is also possible, but generally only when student teachers have established themselves with classes and have shown themselves to be basically competent. At this time, probably towards the end of their course, they are likely to be more confident about their own teaching and able to take in what you are doing:

- *Understanding teaching* – gaining access to your craft knowledge through observation of your actions, informed by a thorough knowledge of the planning, and probably through discussion of the lesson afterwards, with a heightened sensitivity because of having joint responsibility for the lesson.

In addition, collaborative teaching offers you as mentor a means of exploring the student teachers' ideas and thinking about teaching.

Planning

Planning with you for a lesson that is to be taught jointly can help the student teachers to learn in a number of ways. Because experienced teachers do not always produce explicit plans for their lessons, student teachers may mistakenly assume that they too 'do not need to plan'. Collaborative teaching may be a way of making the mentor's planning more explicit and, therefore, accessible to the student teacher, and of demonstrating to the student teacher the necessity of careful plans.

EXAMPLE The need for careful plans

In planning a session of question and answer that was to serve as a recap on the previous week's work, the mentor and student teacher planned even the specific questions that would be asked and considered likely pupil responses. This particular lesson came very near the beginning of the student teacher's time in school, and the thorough discussion was to ensure that the student teacher's questions would be clear to the pupils and pitched at an appropriate level. The planning gave the student teacher the opportunity to learn from the mentor's experience of effective types of question. It also encouraged the student teacher to plan very precisely (in the early stages of learning to teach) to ensure that she did not dry up, or encounter a discouraging sea of blank faces in response to inappropriately phrased questions.

In planning with the student teacher, you can also share your knowledge of the particular class and context. It might be your knowledge of how long a particular task would take different individuals, so reminding the student teacher of the need to develop extension activities for some. Even if your department has clearly defined schemes of work and sets of prepared resources to accompany these, collaborative planning with you can be very useful to show a student teacher how an experienced teacher fleshes out an outline plan and adapts resources to the particular context in which a topic is to be taught.

Learning classroom teaching skills

In the early stages of their course, collaborative teaching can offer the student teacher a protected environment in which to begin developing the skills of classroom teaching. By teaching alongside the student teacher, you can remove some of the fear about maintaining discipline. More importantly, by taking responsibility for certain parts of the lesson, you can enable the student teacher to concentrate on and practise specific aspects of teaching and so build up confidence.

EXAMPLE Practising question and answer

A history student teacher was very anxious to improve her skills of question and answer following a very depressing experience with a class the week before. In this case the mentor deliberately steered the planning for the lesson to ensure that the student teacher led a short session of well-planned question and answer near the beginning of the lesson. She was thus able to focus on this particular aspect without having to worry about the lesson as a whole.

EXAMPLE Developing confidence

A lesson early in the year involved a short debate with student teacher and mentor presenting opposite sides of an argument 'in role'. The student teacher in this case found that assuming a role, and being able to feed off the mentor's arguments, gave her more confidence in front of the whole class and helped her in assuming the 'role' of a teacher (ie, recognizing the element of performance involved in teaching).

EXAMPLE Acquiring a more complex skill

A science student teacher, at a much later stage in the year, was trying to address the issue of differentiated learning – the setting of tasks appropriate to pupils of different abilities. Her mentor helped her begin to explore this by teaching a practical lesson with her. This gave her the confidence and practical help she still needed to set up a range of different experiments.

Understanding teaching

The student teachers' observation of your teaching will be more sharply focused because, having been part of the planning process, they know what you are trying to achieve. They will be able to see what you do to attain your objectives and they will also be aware of any adaptations that you may make to the agreed plan. Knowledge of the original plan should prompt questions about your decision to change things in the lesson and your reasons for doing so. (Obviously changes should only be made if they are not going to disrupt parts of the lesson for which a student teacher is responsible.)

EXAMPLE Appreciating the need for flexibility

In an English lesson, the mentor felt that the discussion that had been set up in small groups had run its course, and altered the activity slightly. The student teacher was only aware of this adaptation because she had been involved in the initial planning. The student teacher's observation of this change led to very fruitful discussion about how the mentor identified priorities at that point.

The benefits for the pupils

Having a student teacher with you in the classroom can:

- allow for a more lively or challenging presentation of information or ideas: eg, role play, debate taking opposing sides

- make the management of learning activities much smoother: eg, having one of you specifically responsible for the distribution of resources while the other explains the task

- increase the amount of individual attention and support that pupils receive: eg, one of you might offer support to specific individuals known to have learning difficulties

- facilitate assessment, or the setting of differentiated tasks: eg one of you might chair a discussion or debate while the other assesses oral contributions.

WHEN TO DO IT

The nature and purpose of collaborative teaching will change as the student teacher progresses. It is therefore important that both you and the student teacher understand why you are using it at any particular point and what you hope to gain from it. It would be inappropriate, for example, to be doing a lot of collaborative teaching at a time when the student teacher is most concerned to develop responsibility for whole classes.

Early on

Collaborative teaching offers student teachers a protected environment in which they can begin to develop the skills of classroom teaching. Here it can give you an opportunity to guide the student teachers' planning and to boost their confidence by sharing responsibility for the lesson as a whole. At this stage, you are likely to retain major responsibility for the class, with the student teacher either in a 'supporting' role working with certain groups of individuals, or taking overall responsibility for short sections of the lesson – exposition, question and answer, or sharing the feedback from group work.

In these early days you should identify with the student teachers what kind of skills it is most useful for them to work on and, to some extent, plan the lesson around these, to allow them the opportunities they need. Below is a list of some of the sorts of skills that student teachers might usefully focus on in a lesson that is taught collaboratively:

- speaking to a whole class – exposition, task-setting
- organizing/chairing a whole-class discussion
- question and answer
- working with slow learners
- providing extension activities and working with more able pupils
- small group work
- use of audio-visual material.

In deciding which skills to focus on at any given time, your thinking should take account of:

- the range of teaching strategies that could be used in teaching your subject
- the programme within the partnership for your particular subject area (this might be a joint programme between you and the university/college)
- the agreed list of interactive teaching competences/skills/qualities.

Later

As the student teachers become more competent they are likely to take a much more central role both in the planning and the teaching. You can then use collaborative teaching to extend their repertoire of teaching strategies:

- Are there certain teaching strategies, eg, role play, or the setting of differentiated activities, which collaborative teaching might allow your student teacher to experiment with, once you are confident that they have acquired basic skills?

- Is there any aspect of teaching that the student teacher is especially eager to develop that could usefully be explored through collaborative teaching?

- Would collaborative teaching prove useful to your student teacher in helping them to plan collaboratively, in preparation for work as part of a 'department team' in their induction year? (Is this an approach to teaching which you, or your student teachers, believe to be valuable in itself, and therefore worth developing more now?)

- Would you and your student teacher enjoy teaching collaboratively, now that you perhaps have more time to plan together, and now that the student teacher feels that they have more to contribute?

- Now that your student teacher is competent, are there particular teaching strategies needing two teachers that you would like to use for the benefit of your pupils?

PUTTING IT INTO PRACTICE

Planning

Effective collaborative teaching demands clear and detailed planning so that both you and the student teacher understand exactly what you are doing. Uncertainty about who is doing what, when, is likely to cause confusion for everyone including the pupils. As the teacher responsible for the lesson you must ensure that the plan and timing are clear. It is especially important that you have an agreed understanding about who is responsible for control and discipline at any particular time. Although this is time-consuming, without it the student teacher might well abdicate certain responsibilities to you or end up feeling thoroughly undermined. An agreed format for recording collaborative teaching plans should help in the planning process. Figure 4.1 provides an example of a completed collaborative teaching plan.

During the lesson

During the lesson itself there may be opportunities for you and the student teacher to discuss aspects of the teaching. The student teacher may want to ask

Figure 4.1 *An example of a completed collaborative teaching plan*

Collaborative Teaching Plan			
Class: *9 CD*		Date: *18th Nov Period 1*	
Topic: *French Revolution: Reforms of Assembly Flight of King & consequences*		Context of the class: *Follows detailed work on causes of Revolution & introduction to reformers' ideas*	
Lesson objectives (ie pupils learning): *Concept of equality Reliability of evidence. (Causation – if enough time.)*		Objectives for student teacher's learning: *Further practice of Q & A. Exposition*	

'Activity' should also make clear exactly how the transitions from one activity to another will be made.

Time	Activity	Mentor's Role	Student Teacher's Role
8·35	Settle class, register	L.S. Register	DP
8·40	Recap/Q&A on homework	} observation	Q&A Exposition
8·50	Exposition – failure of King's escape		
8·55	Introduce sources to examine Louis' reasons. Q&A – reliability	Q&A to introduce issues. Discuss reliability	} Observation
9·00	Exercise on worksheet. Fast finishers – questions on why he failed.	Explain task. Distribute worksheets. Help individuals as necessary & direct them on to new task.	Help distribute worksheets. Help individuals direct to new task. observation
9·20?	If time – causes & consequences exercise in groups		
9·30	Wind up	Explain & help End lesson – recap	Collect worksheets.

It should be clear what each will be doing at any particular point.

Resources needed	Whose responsibility	Focus of observation
Worksheet of Sources on reason for escape	L.S	Q&A Exposition
Cards for causes/consequences	L.S	
Textbooks	D.P	

This box may be used to specify what the mentor or student teacher should be observing if there are times when they are not actively involved in the teaching.

Time agreed to evaluate lesson:

about something they have just seen you do, or you may want to offer brief feedback on their teaching, or offer guidance on the next stage of the plan given the way in which the class has responded so far. This kind of discussion can be a very valuable part of the process, and you may wish to plan the lesson deliberately to allow opportunities for this – when pupils are working individually or in groups, for example. A word of warning: such discussions are not always possible and it is helpful anyway to keep them brief, so that the pupils do not perceive you and the student teacher to be 'chatting' while they are working!

Debriefing

From the student teachers' point of view, it is most useful if the lesson can be followed by discussion. It is worth allowing about 15 minutes for evaluation afterwards, and preferably within the next 24 hours. The nature of the discussion will vary according to the student teachers' needs and stage of development, but it should provide opportunities for the student teachers to ask about those parts of the lessons that you taught as well as giving you a chance to provide feedback on their teaching. (The materials on 'Opening up your practice' – Unit 5, and 'Diagnostic assessment and supervision' – Unit 3, are obviously relevant here.)

COLLEAGUES WORKING WITH STUDENT TEACHERS

Collaborative teaching does require time for planning and for debriefing, but it can be a very rewarding experience for teacher and pupils as well for the student teachers. You may well find, therefore, that some of your colleagues would welcome working collaboratively with the student teachers. To help your colleagues work in this way you could:

- use department meeting time to discuss together some of the points outlined in these materials

- encourage the use of an agreed format for collaborative planning.

- with individual colleagues discuss particular skills that they could help the student teachers to develop through collaborative teaching.

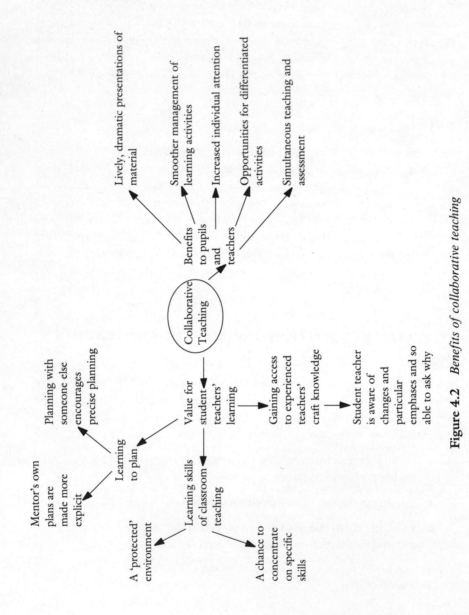

Figure 4.2 *Benefits of collaborative teaching*

Summary

Collaborative teaching benefits

- *student teachers*

- *teachers*

- *pupils.*

These benefits are summarized in Figure 4.2. To do it well you need:

- *time – for joint planning and debriefing*

- *a clear plan – in which objectives, activities, responsibility for resources, and the roles of mentor and student teacher at each point are clearly understood*

- *a specific purpose – because of the time demands, think carefully about how its use will benefit the student teacher's learning at any particular point.*

UNIT 5

OPENING UP YOUR PRACTICE: GIVING STUDENT TEACHERS ACCESS TO YOUR PROFESSIONAL CRAFT KNOWLEDGE

Student teachers have much to learn from observing you and your colleagues, but it seems that the more skilful the teaching, the easier everything looks, and the more difficult it is for observers to appreciate the complexities of classroom life and understand how success is achieved. They may, indeed, misunderstand what is going on if they are not thinking about the class and the teaching in the same way the teacher is. Student teachers can, however, achieve a much fuller understanding of a particular lesson, if, following observation, they have an opportunity to discuss the lesson with the teacher. The teacher then has the opportunity to talk about the kinds of pupil activities and progress he or she was aiming to promote, the actions taken to bring these about and the conditions impinging on the teaching which had to be taken into account when deciding what to do. One of the most valuable ways in which you can help student teachers to understand the complexities of classroom teaching and to learn more about teachers' skill, strategies and achievements in the classroom is through observation with follow-up discussion.

THE IMPORTANCE OF OBSERVATION WITH FOLLOW-UP INTERVIEW

Observation without discussion – the limitations

Picture the following scene.

A Year 9 class. The pupils are arranged in groups of four or five, and are exploring the notion of Standard English. In each group, one of the pupils is chairing the discussion, while another is recording the group's conclusions. The teacher moves from group to group, occasionally standing at the back or at the side of the class looking on. All the pupils are on task, and the noise level is low.

It would be very easy for an observer – especially one with no experience of teaching – to assume that the learning that took place in the lesson had nothing to do with the teacher, and that she was simply fortunate to find herself working with such a well-motivated and self-disciplined set of pupils. There is, however, a lot more to teaching than meets the eye. Experienced teachers often make skilful teaching look easy: problems are anticipated and, because of actions taken to avoid or prevent them, do not become apparent.

Teachers' professional craft knowledge

Teachers themselves are inclined to take many of their teaching skills for granted. When, for example, they are approached by would-be observers, they tend to dismiss their day-to-day teaching by apologising for 'ordinary lessons' with little of interest to be observed. (In fact, what can seem ordinary, everyday, familiar, routine aspects of teaching to the teacher with several years' experience in the classroom may be a source of anxiety to the beginning teacher.) In the same vein, a common response to an observer commenting on the success of a lesson is to give credit to the pupils – 'they're a good class, they don't need teaching'.

Teachers are used to having conversations about teaching in general, their pupils, the school and so on, but they are rarely, if ever, asked to talk about the knowledge and expertise acquired through experience that guides their day-to-day practice. However, one of the most valuable sources of knowledge for student teachers is the knowledge embedded in the teacher's actual practice – the teacher's taken-for-granted craft knowledge. Student teachers, therefore, need opportunities to get behind the scenes of observed lessons, to find out how the teacher saw a particular lesson, and why the teacher did what he or she did.

WHY DO IT?

The benefits for the student teachers' learning

- This type of observation with follow-up interview focusing on the specifics of the lesson observed can give student teachers rich insights into the fine grain of teaching.

It is especially valuable in giving them insights into the many conditions that teachers take account of. As one mentor commented after a number of observations with follow-up interview:

They certainly helped Paul begin to understand that what we did in a lesson depended on so many things – the class, what sorts of things I was trying to get them to learn, the kinds of lessons we'd been having earlier, everything, even down to the weather. It also helped him to see how alert you have to be, how you're constantly fine-tuning what's going on as things unravel during the lesson.

The following short extracts from four lengthy conversations between student teachers and their mentors do not do justice to the richness of the mentors' craft knowledge, but they are useful in illustrating the nature of this kind of conversation following an observed lesson.

EXAMPLE The complexity of ordinary teaching

1. *Student: I noticed your instructions were incredibly clear.*
   Mentor: That's nice, because as I was writing them on the board, and rubbing bits off to get other bits in, I was thinking, this is not ideal board work. Yes, but I hope – with this class in particular, it needs to be spelled out to them absolutely clearly what they have to do. There are people there who wander off very easily, and who forget things. So with them, I write things down – one, two, three, what they've got to do, and then they've got 10 minutes to look at it on the board, and hopefully no one will forget.

2. *Student: Could you say a bit more about whether it turned out as you wanted it to – did it go according to plan?*
   Mentor: In a situation like that, on that occasion, that's the way I wanted it to be. It's a last lesson on a Tuesday, they're not particularly interested in looking through documents on navvies. But I wanted to deal with those documents with them, and because of that, and because it fitted into that point of the course, I did it that way. On another occasion, in different circumstances, I would've given them the work to do in groups to report back – maybe if it had been first lesson on a Friday.

continued overleaf

3. Student: I was very interested in the pupil-pupil discussion which I thought was really good and it's the first time that I've seen pupils split up like that for discussion for 15 minutes or so.

   Teacher: Thank you. Well, the idea was that it was a new topic – Venn diagrams – and I was trying to get them to think about how else they could show that kind of information. I could have just said what I said at the beginning, but I felt that they ought to think for themselves, and the only way they can really gain by that I think is to bounce ideas off each other because it's very difficult – they find it difficult anyway. But it's even more difficult stuck there by yourself thinking 'I haven't got any ideas at all!'. A few of them did come up with ideas because they were able to ask each other

4. Student: The first question – and this is something I think is really important – is how did you ensure that there was no shouting out when you asked a question, you know, set of questions?

   Teacher: I think it depends on how many ground rules you've actually set up right from, right from the start with any particular group. I mean you need to decide what, I suppose what kind of atmosphere and what kind of behaviour you'll, you are prepared to accept from a class, kind of running right through the time you're going to be teaching them. And you just have to set that up right from the very start and I think you just do a lot of hard work once you've decided what's acceptable and what's not; you do a lot of hard work at the beginning of any course actually explaining those ground rules to them, and reinforcing them on every conceivable occasion. I mean you may have noticed this morning that I did actually remind them before we even started that the only acceptable way of sharing contributions was for me to be asking one individual at a time and for them to be, to put hands up and wait to be asked.

■ Observation with follow-up interview can help to demystify classroom teaching, to break it down in such a way that various skills become learnable.

EXAMPLE Understanding how

A student teacher wanted to be able to achieve the calm working atmosphere that her mentor had with the same class. She knew what the desirable classroom atmosphere looked like, but she had no idea how it was achieved, and therefore could not learn how to achieve it (or how to create that kind of atmosphere in her own lessons).

In a discussion following observation of her mentor – in the course of asking her specific questions about the observed lesson – she learned that her mentor had spent a long time establishing ways of behaviour in the classroom, and had seen it as a priority at the beginning of the year; that she was holding the class on a fairly tight rein because she felt that they could easily get over-excited; and that she had spent a long time working with an individual pupil because he had been away and had missed what the mentor saw as a core lesson. These and other insights helped the student teacher to see what was behind the atmosphere she wanted in her lessons, and she was now able to set about learning how to achieve it.

■ Giving student teachers access to *why*, can help them to understand the *what* and the *how*.

EXAMPLE Discovering why

A science student was struck by the fact that with one particular Year 11 class, his mentor ended every lesson with a spelling test. He assumed that the mentor was very concerned with the pupils' spelling, and was surprised to find out that the tests were being used as a control mechanism with a class that could get 'sloppy' towards the end of a double period. The teacher used the test to keep the pace of the lesson going until the end and to ensure that it ended in an orderly way – as well as to ensure the pupils could spell key words.

The benefits for you

Having to think about your classroom teaching in this way really makes you appreciate the skills you have. It can also encourage you to build on those skills, to refine the techniques you use or to develop new ways of doing things. Below are the comments of two mentors who are enthusiastic about opening up their practice in this way.

EXAMPLE Recognizing and developing your own skills

1. Talking after a lesson about why I'd done things, what I was trying to achieve, what I was pleased with etc, has helped me to develop self-evaluation skills. I find it much easier now to analyse what I'm doing. Not only that, I'm more interested in analysing my own teaching, and I think I'm a better teacher for it.

2. I've become a lot more interested in developing my own classroom practice because of talking with my student in this way. Before, I really didn't realize how much went into teaching, and in some ways I think I'd lost sight of some things. Anyway, I think it's a good thing – I actually enjoy looking back on the lesson and really thinking about what was going on.

The benefits for your department or faculty

Working in this way with student teachers can help you and your faculty colleagues learn from each other's expertise. As well as fostering an atmosphere in which you can talk openly about the teaching of particular lessons, it can encourage you to watch each other's lessons with a view to learning from each other.

EXAMPLE Encouraging openness

After a while, the way you work with students is bound to spill over onto the way you work with other teachers. We got used to talking about our teaching with the students and it somehow became more natural to have the same kind of conversation with other teachers – talking about specific teaching strategies and what we saw as our strengths and weaknesses. We became much more aware of the things that different people were good at, and we became more open about asking each other for help.

PREPARING THE STUDENT TEACHERS

The student teachers' understanding

As discussed in Unit 2, Observation, student teachers need guidance about the purpose of any observation. This is particularly so when, as in this case, they have a vital part to play in the whole process. The way they go about the follow-up interview can make a real difference to the teacher's ability to reveal the thinking behind the lesson. To help them appreciate the value of this kind of observation, it is worth talking with them about the nature of classroom teaching and the processes involved in learning to teach. To learn from the professional craft knowledge of you and other teachers, they have to be convinced of the need to:

- **Think beyond the next lesson**
  Through getting access to the professional craft knowledge of you or one of your colleagues they may well acquire skills that they can add to their developing repertoires. It is just as likely, however, that they will learn skills and strategies that they cannot put into immediate use in their practice and will need to tuck away for use later in their training or when they are qualified. Above all, a developed under-standing of your everyday practice can help them to understand teaching and to develop their own ways of thinking.

- **Focus on particular aspects of teaching**
  Many student teachers start off with a broad but superficial view of teaching, categorizing teachers according to their overall style and personality. This leads them to believe that they can learn only from someone whose overall style of teaching they find attractive and wish to emulate. You can help them to understand that effective classroom teaching demands that one can work in a number of ways. By looking at the particular techniques teachers use to achieve certain effects – the component parts of their teaching – rather than being distracted by overall teaching 'styles', they will be able to learn much that is useful.

- **Recognize that classroom teaching is complex**
  When they recognize that general 'rules of thumb' such as 'Don't smile 'til Christmas' are of limited value, and that skilled teaching depends on taking account of a multitude of conditions in each situation, they can truly appreciate how much there is to be learned from the teaching of experienced practitioners.

- **Set aside their own ways of thinking**
  In the follow-up interview student teachers may be anxious to talk about how they saw the lesson and to put their own interpretation on what they saw. They need to set aside their assumptions and preconceptions and be prepared to listen to the ways in which you construe classroom situations and events.

Preparing for observation

To ensure that the student teachers learn as much as possible from this process of observation with follow-up interview, it is helpful to:

- **Decide on the focus of observation**
  During the first few weeks of their time in school, you will need to decide on the focus of observation, which is likely to be everyday classroom management skills such as:

  - introducing the work of the day to the class

  - beginning and ending a lesson

  - the transition from whole-class to group activity

  - dealing with unexpected pupil behaviour or interruptions

  - maintaining or establishing relationships with particular pupils.

  As the student teachers' understanding of classrooms and of teaching grows, and as they begin to develop their own practice, it is useful to get them to focus on any aspects of teaching that they find especially challenging.

  Towards the end of their training when they are learning how to evaluate their teaching in the light of their own criteria, the student teachers will be in a position to take the initiative in determining the focus of observation.

- **Put the student teachers in the picture**
  Before the lesson give the student teachers some background information about the class to be observed – the work they have been doing, individual pupils, aims of the lesson and so on. By putting the lesson into its context in this way you are giving them more of a chance to observe intelligently.

EXAMPLE Providing the necessary context

I said, 'This is the sort of thing I'm going to do' and went through the lesson plan with her and explained that this was the plan and told her and gave her contingency plans – 'If they take ages' and 'If they finish too early'. And we talked about the kinds of things I was trying to get out of it.

- **Sort out the timing of the follow-up interview**
  When the lesson is fresh in your mind you are likely to have a lot to

say about it. The sooner the discussion takes place after the lesson, therefore, the more useful it is likely to be. If possible, allow 10–15 minutes for the discussion.

- **Remind the student teachers of the purpose of the observation**
  Make sure that they understand that they are concentrating on your perspective: what you, as teacher, were faced with; what you were doing and what you were achieving. Emphasize the importance of acknowledging that as observers they cannot know what is going on in your mind and, therefore, during the lesson they need to make notes of the questions they wish to ask you and of the situations to which they refer.

Preparing for the follow-up interview

In the normal course of events teachers are rarely, if ever, asked to talk about the knowledge they use in teaching particular lessons. To peel away the layers of understanding and to reveal the knowledge embedded in the teaching of an individual lesson is not always easy, especially when you are not used to doing it. The right kind of questions, prompts and probes from the student teachers can help you to reveal your thinking. You will, however, need to guide them in how to conduct the interview if you are to avoid the following kind of exchange in which the teacher, far from opening up his practice, was immediately put on the defensive by questions which implied criticism of his teaching:

Student: *Is that what you wanted to happen?*
Teacher: *Is what – sorry, I'm not sure what you mean?*
Student: *Well. They didn't actually get round to making any notes did they?*
Teacher: *Um, well, they had lots of good ideas and I felt they were all involved in the lesson.*
Student: *Why didn't you split up that group at the back?*
Teacher: *!!!*

To get at the thinking behind the teaching the student teachers should concentrate on what went well in the lesson and ask questions which encourage the teacher to explain rather than to justify what he or she did.

Encourage them to ask questions that focus on:

- what went well in the lesson

- the actions taken by the teacher that made things go well

- the teacher's reasons for doing what she or he did.

Remind them that their questions can help teachers talk about the ordinary, everyday things that they usually take for granted. They should therefore:

- be prepared to ask follow-up questions before moving on to a new topic. They should never be shy of saying, 'Can you tell me a little more about that?'

- ask open questions which invite the teacher to reveal her or his thinking in the lesson rather than closed questions looking for confirmation or denial of what the student teacher thinks

- ask questions about the particular lesson rather than broad questions about teaching in general.

Help them to understand that to get at the teacher's thinking in the lesson they will need to be self-disciplined in the discussion. They should resist the temptation to talk about their own teaching or to swap anecdotes with the teacher. To help student teachers learn as much as possible from this process, it is worth offering them some detailed notes of guidance. As an example of how this might be done, Figure 5.1 reproduces the notes given to student teachers within the school-based course at Oxford.

WHEN TO DO IT

Observation with follow-up interview of the kind outlined above can, of course, take place at any time during training. It can, however, be an especially valuable way of helping student teachers to develop both their understanding and their skills, once they have acquired some experience of classroom teaching. In the words of an experienced mentor:

> As a student teacher you need to have done something, then to go back and observe, because it's only when you've done it, you realize what it's about, where the problems are, and you see how other people solve them. It's as if you need to know enough to know what you don't know – at first it can all look very easy or perhaps overwhelming.

When the student teachers are in a position to take the initiative in deciding what they need to learn – normally towards the end of their training – and can identify areas of their practice they wish to strengthen and develop, it is very helpful if you can point them to particular teachers in the school – irrespective of their subject – who are especially skilled in those areas.

EXAMPLE Observing an appropriate teacher

A history student was anxious to improve the way in which she worked with a class that was generally regarded as of 'low ability'. She found it very difficult to get them to work, and was troubled by the kind of teacher she was becoming with them – strident, moaning, frustrated, gloomy. Her mentor suggested she observe an English teacher who was known throughout the school as outstanding at motivating pupils that others saw as reluctant learners. It worked. As a result of observation and follow-up interview with the teacher, she began to understand what was going wrong for her with a similar group, and what she could do to improve matters.

Figure 5.1   *Notes of guidance for student teachers*

OBSERVING TEACHERS AT WORK: MAKING SENSE OF WHAT THEY DO

Interviewing the teacher after the lesson: some suggestions

1. It is generally useful to ask questions that focus on:

   ■ the teacher's successes or achievements
      One way of starting is by asking the teacher what he or she was
      pleased with in the lesson.

   ■ the actions taken by the teacher to achieve those things
      eg, *'I noticed that everyone managed to do the experiment. How did
      you get that to happen?'*
      *'You said that you were pleased that a lot more people than usual
      contributed to class discussion today. What did you do to bring that
      about?'*

   ■ the teacher's reasons for taking the action he or she did
      eg, *'Can you tell me why you asked the groups to report back in that
      way?'*

   ■ the conditions, circumstances, etc, that led to the teacher making a
      decision to take a particular action
      eg, *'You said that they had had enough of the reading, and so you
      moved on to the questions. How did you know that they'd had enough,
      how could you tell?'*

2. In the discussion or follow-up interview you can help the teacher to talk
about the ordinary, everyday things that s/he usually takes for granted.
Never be afraid of saying, 'Could you tell me a little more about that?'
eg, Student: *You said that you were pleased because the noise level was just right.
           Can you tell me how you judged that it was right?*
   Teacher: *It's a balance, isn't it? The atmosphere is there, but the work is there
           as well. I was happy with the balance today. It's personal, hard to say.*
At this point, instead of moving on to another aspect of the lesson, it would be
helpful to ask:
   Student: *Can you talk a little more about the balance, and say something
           about how you knew when it was the right balance?*

3. Try not to ask your questions in a generalized way. You are more likely
to get answers of interest to you if relate your questions to the *particular*
lesson observed.

eg, *How did you manage to get Patrick and Clare to work?*
   rather than
   What do you do to persuade unwilling pupils to work?
The first question is much more likely to lead to the teacher talking about their actual practice, in the lesson observed and with other classes.

4. Try to stick to the point.
Remember that your job is to seek information from the teacher, which means asking them questions about what you saw in the particular lesson observed. Try to avoid talking about your own teaching.

5. Most teachers are not used to being asked questions about what they did in a lesson and why, and they may feel a little anxious at first. Be sensitive to these anxieties, particularly in the way you ask questions.
For instance, a closed question which invites a yes/no answer does not help a respondent to give an informative reply. More important, it may also convey implications of what the teacher should or should not have done, and so have undertones of criticism. A question such as, 'Did you have a lesson plan?' would tend to put any teacher on the defensive.

6. Avoid attempting to test your own ideas and assumptions about what you saw in the lesson – keep the questions open.
eg, *'Did you cut short the question and answer session because you felt they were beginning to get confused?'*
   is not as helpful as:
   'Can you tell me why you cut short the question and answer session?'

7. Never ask, 'Why didn't you...?'
This is almost guaranteed to lead teachers to justify their teaching rather than to reveal their thinking.

A successful discussion is one in which:

- the teacher does most of the talking

- the teacher explains her/his actions but does not feel the need to justify them

- the questions are rooted in the observed lesson

- the focus is on what went well in the lesson

- you learn much more than you could have done simply from observing the lesson.

SUMMARY

Skilful teaching looks easy. Observation alone *will not enable your student teachers to recognize how complex effective teaching is and to understand how success in the classroom is achieved. Observation with follow-up interview offers a way for student teachers to get 'behind the scenes' of a lesson — to find out:*

- *how the teacher saw things*
- *what the teacher was trying to achieve*
- *why the teacher adopted a particular course of action.*

A successful follow-up interview is one in which your student teachers allow you to talk about:

- *the thinking behind your actions*
- *the kinds of learning and behaviour you were trying to promote*
- *the actions you took to achieve your aims*
- *the conditions or circumstances which impinged on your teaching or that you had to take into account when deciding what to do.*

UNIT 6

CRITICALLY DISCUSSING STUDENT TEACHERS' IDEAS

All student teachers as they begin their training bring with them a wealth of ideas about teaching and learning – ideas significantly influenced by their own experience of education. Their beliefs and expectations will determine their priorities and influence what they consider they will need to learn. They will also be bringing into school ideas from other sources: university/college tutors, reading about educational research and national developments, fellow students.

To gain as much as possible from their time in school, student teachers need to be made aware of the ideas they hold about teaching – wherever they have come from – and be given opportunities to discuss and critically evaluate them. In helping student teachers learn to teach, you therefore need to encourage them to articulate their ideas, both in general terms and as they relate to specific lessons. You can then help student teachers begin to question these ideas, seeking to establish through discussion, as well as observation and practice, whether they are helpful or valid.

WHY IS IT IMPORTANT?

Student teachers arrive full of ideas

All student teachers bring with them their own, often very strong, ideas about teaching and learning (they are unlikely otherwise to want to become teachers!). They will have encountered a range of assumptions and ideas about teaching:

- in the university/college part of their training course

- through observation in other schools, perhaps undertaken at the start of their course

- through their own experience of education as pupils in schools and as students in higher education.

Just as any teacher encountering a new group or embarking on a new topic seeks to establish what their pupils already know and perhaps what opinions they hold about the topic, so it is important for you to appreciate that student teachers do not come to you as 'empty vessels waiting to be filled'.

Those ideas which derive from university/college may be much easier to bring into the open: they may be stated on the curriculum programme, and may have been discussed by you and the university/college tutor in planning the student teachers' programme. However, those ideas which student teachers bring with them from their own experience as pupils or students are perhaps more difficult to expose and analyse; they are also much more deep-rooted and difficult to change.

Critical learners, not clones

There is no one way to teach. Different approaches work for different people in different circumstances and in different ways. The purpose of any training course is not simply to produce teachers who can perform effectively in the classroom, but to allow student teachers to learn about teaching, to explore different strategies, and to discover what kind of teacher they want to be. This kind of learning can only happen if student teachers are made aware of the range of possible approaches open to them, and are helped to assess the implications of adopting different strategies.

If, when they first go into schools, rather than as they complete their course, student teachers could recognize and begin to evaluate their own preconceptions and the ideas they bring from elsewhere, they would be able to make much more effective use of their time in school. You therefore have a crucial task in devising ways of bringing student teachers' ideas out into the open, and in helping them to subject those ideas to serious questioning.

WHAT MAKES IT DIFFICULT?

The pace of school life

Teachers are extremely busy people. You are under constant pressure to deliver lessons day in and day out. During the average school day it is virtually impossible to find the time or space to think beyond the next lesson or meeting. Once student teachers begin to teach, even small groups or parts of a lesson, the priority for discussion with you automatically becomes planning for the next lesson. Such conversations have a very specific focus, and are inevitably dominated by the need to produce something concrete for the lesson. They do not often involve discussion at a more general level – the purpose of teaching a particular subject, the value of mixed-ability teaching, for example – where the student teachers' ideas can be explored and questioned without the need for an 'answer' to solve an immediate problem. It is all too easy for mentor and student teachers to be pressurized into 'short-term thinking' and to lose sight of the longer-term perspective, and any sense of the fact that the course is only the beginning of the student teacher's learning process as a teacher. As one science mentor observed:

> It's important to use the fact that student teachers do have time to think, to discuss, to question, to observe – to learn really. It's all too easy to get them snarled up in the frantic pace of school, unable to look beyond 10Y's next lesson. Sometimes, a conscious effort has to be made to get the student teacher to resist the pressure to think only in terms of what you've got to do tomorrow.

Student teachers' confidence

Student teachers need to learn how to question their ideas about teaching from the beginning of their course. However, they can feel very insecure at this time and only really develop the confidence to subject their ideas to serious critical analysis when they have found their feet. You therefore have to strike a delicate balance. This avoids the problem experienced by a maths mentor who described his student teacher as having 'developed a complacent smugness that effectively sealed him off from any serious questioning and brought his learning to an abrupt halt'.

SOME WAYS OF DOING IT

The ideas that student teachers have about teaching and learning will present themselves in two different ways:

- *wide-ranging conversations about teaching in general* – discussing the kind of role they believe teachers should have with their classes, or the relative merits of groupwork as a teaching strategy, for example.

- *focused discussion related to particular lessons* – planning or evaluating a lesson of their own, or discussing their observation of a lesson taught by you. In the teaching strategies they adopt or in the comments they make it is possible to discern a great deal about student teachers' views of different approaches to teaching.

Exploring general ideas

Through discussion

This requires careful planning. For student teachers spontaneously to articulate and evaluate their general ideas about teaching and learning is unusual. It is worth setting aside time very early on in their stay with you, before the student teachers become preoccupied with planning for particular lessons, to find out what kind of ideas they bring with them:

- What kind of teachers had most influence upon them, and perhaps upon their decision to take up teaching?

- What did they dislike most about their own schooling?

- Why do they believe their subject to be important?

- How do they perceive their own role as a teacher – as leader? counsellor? facilitator? entertainer?

An appreciation of the ideas that your particular student teachers bring with them is invaluable to you, and may save considerable time later on.

Through observation and debriefing

In observing student teachers over a period of time you can gauge a great deal about their priorities and their views on teaching and learning styles. Helping them to question these assumptions can be done in a variety of ways.

EXAMPLE Building confidence before challenging

One history mentor was aware from discussions early on that her student teacher had quite a 'traditional' view of the teacher's role: 'she came with the idea firmly fixed in her head that a good teacher commanded silence in class, stood at the front and taught content'. She judged that it would be inappropriate to challenge that model too forcefully early on as it lay at the heart of the student teacher's beliefs about good teaching. So, instead of criticizing the student teacher for wanting to teach in that kind of way she did two things. She allowed the student teacher to plan and teach a number of lessons in line with that model, knowing that once the student teacher felt confident in her ability to fulfil that role, she would be able to look beyond it and question the adequacy of the model. At the same time the mentor also ensured that the student teacher was continually exposed to other possible approaches. In the words of the mentor, 'Mary (the student teacher) observed a lot of my lessons and I always shared my lesson plans and talked about pupil activities. In discussing the plan, I would always try to slip in the fact that I chose tasks specifically to teach particular concepts and skills, and not merely to get across the historical content'.

With some student teachers it can be counterproductive to question directly what they are doing. On those occasions it can be helpful for you simply to collect data for them to examine.

EXAMPLE Using data to prompt questions

In one case a student teacher set out with the aim of being a friend to her pupils, being liked as a teacher. The mentor, concerned about the implications of this approach, simply noted a number of the remarks made to the student teacher by pupils in the course of a lesson and showed them to her as part of the debriefing. Reflecting on the remarks herself, the student teacher began to question the approach and ask for advice on ways to create a different pupil/teacher relationship.

This technique of data collection can prove one way of tackling over-confident, even arrogant, student teachers who will not accept that there is another point of view, or that their approach is not necessarily 'the best'. By providing objective data – the written work of classes taught the same topic in different ways, for example – you can force the student teachers to confront the issue and question the validity of their assumptions.

Through awareness of other aspects of the student teachers' course

If the school or university/college runs a general programme alongside the work of subject-specific mentors, this may be an important source of ideas which student teachers bring to their curriculum work. Awareness of the issues being tackled at any given time can alert you to particular issues that your student teachers may be wrestling with. This does not require detailed knowledge of what the sessions cover, but if you know that your student teachers have been discussing equal opportunities or special needs, for example, you can perhaps ask about the conclusions they reached or how they might influence their next lesson plan.

Exploring ideas relating to specific lessons

In this context it is relatively easy to encourage student teachers to share the ideas from their experience or from university/college which have influenced their thinking. Here you play a significant role in:

- helping student teachers to clarify their ideas

- encouraging them to assess the likely implications of particular strategies

- giving them opportunities to try out or test their ideas. You need to make sure that the student teacher(s) question the ideas they are considering using.

EXAMPLE Questioning ideas from other sources

A geography teacher, when being taken through a student teacher's lesson plan, was intrigued by the choice of role play for that particular class. Through getting the student teacher to talk about his reasons for the choice, it became apparent to the mentor that the student teacher had recently read a book extolling the virtues of role play in geography and was unquestioningly adopting it without considering the needs of that particular group.

As the student teachers plan, questions about what exactly will be happening are usually the most helpful way of getting them to clarify their ideas. On group-work for example:

- How are you going to decide who's in which group?

- Does everyone in the group have to write down their decisions?

- When they are reporting back, how interested is everyone else in the class going to be in hearing what somebody else is saying?

Such questions serve not only to clarify the plan – to help student teachers realize exactly what needs to be done – but also to alert them to the potential problems as well as benefits of certain approaches. Thoughtful questioning about the methods that the student teachers are planning to use can help to spell out the fact that there is no such thing as a good teaching strategy in itself. The value of any particular approach must be judged in terms of what the teacher is trying to achieve.

Summary

Student teachers bring with them ideas shaped by their own education and from the university/college-based parts of their course. Just as pupils' learning is so much more effective when we take account of the knowledge and ideas that they bring with them to the subject, so student teachers' learning can be accelerated by taking time to explore their preconceptions. If you can help student teachers to question their own assumptions and those of others from the very beginning of the course, they will develop much more quickly into reflective practitioners rather than simply competent teachers. You can encourage this questioning:

- *through general discussion of student teachers' ideas about teaching and learning*

- *through observation and debriefing of specific lessons.*

To do it well you need to:

- *make time to explore the student teachers' preconceptions. Avoid the pressure to confine discussion simply to the next lesson to be taught*

- *strike a balance — encourage the student teachers to air their ideas without letting them think that they already have all the answers; question the student teachers' ideas without crushing their confidence*

- *provide the student teachers with data collected from observation of their lessons to allow them to assess the practical implication of their ideas.*

SUPPORTING STUDENT TEACHERS' SELF-EVALUATION

As student teachers progress and become more experienced and skilful, they will naturally take on more responsibility, become more involved in various aspects of school life and increasingly take the initiative in terms of their own learning. In the first phase of their learning, through diagnostic assessment their performance is evaluated in the light of an agreed list of teaching qualities/competences/skills. Once they have shown themselves to be competent, they will be ready to enter a second phase of their learning in which the emphasis is properly on self-evaluation and reflection. Without abandoning the basic standard of competency, in this second phase they have the opportunity to identify what is important to them as teachers and to concentrate on those aspects of their teaching which they are most concerned to develop. The agenda is now theirs rather than yours but you have an important role in helping them to clarify and develop their thinking.

WHY DO IT?

While it is important that new entrants to the profession should have attained basic competence in classroom teaching, it is at least equally important that they should go on learning and improving once they become teachers. Probably all teachers *do* go on learning, but for many, especially in the early habit-forming years, this learning can be of a trial-and-error kind, mainly directed towards coping with the many and immediate demands of the job. If teachers are to be educational thinkers whose thinking informs, and is informed by, their learning about classroom teaching, then the foundations for this are best laid when they are student teachers. That means helping them to develop the skills and habits necessary for relating their classroom practice to their educational aspirations: enabling them to become self-developing professionals through learning how to evaluate and to improve their own practice. During their training course student teachers will be able to focus on no more than one or two significant aspects of their teaching. What is important, however, is that they should acquire the attitudes, skills and confidence necessary to engage in this kind of self-evaluation throughout their teaching career.

TWO PHASES OF LEARNING

During the first phase of your student teachers' learning, your concern, in collaboration with the university tutor or with a co-assessor in school, is with evaluating their performance. In the second phase, the student teachers should take responsibility for evaluating their own performance. This is not to say that until this point student teachers have relied solely on you for judgement about their teaching competence. Diagnostic assessment, as used in the first phase, is usually most productive when student teachers are encouraged to reflect on the positive and negative aspects of a lesson for themselves before you contribute your judgements, and indeed the suggested pattern is intended to encourage the student teachers to analyse their own performance. However, in the first phase the criteria against which student teachers are encouraged to analyse their teaching are externally imposed by the list of teaching qualities/competences/ skills agreed by the partnership, and judgement about whether they have achieved competence in relation to them is made by you, in collaboration with the tutor from the university/college or school co-assessor.

However, if student teachers are to progress beyond mere competency it is important that their vision of good teaching should not be permanently constrained by an externally imposed set of criteria. In the second phase, which in a PGCE course is likely to begin about two-thirds of the way through the year, they have the chance to think about their own ideals as teachers and to select or develop their own criteria by which to judge the effectiveness of their own teaching. This means that it is the student teacher who determines the focus of your lesson observation and the data to be collected from it.

Diagnostic assessment has now given way to partnership supervision. The feedback that you give after a lesson consists of the data collected during your observation, which you explain if necessary, but do not evaluate. Responsibility for evaluation – drawing conclusions about the efficacy of their teaching and ways to improve it – now rests with the student teachers. However, since this process is extremely demanding, you have a vital role to play in helping them to interpret and use the data. Your task is to support them in their self-evaluation.

WHAT DOES IT INVOLVE?

The whole process of self-evaluation involves you and the student teachers in:

- discussion to identify the focuses of the evaluation

- observation of their lessons

- non-judgemental feedback on the observed lessons (partnership supervision).

The process of self-evaluation will also involve the student teachers in:

- exploring the literature on the aspects of teaching that they are especially interested in

- observing and discussing experienced teachers' practice (including your own).

Helping student teachers identify areas of interest

You can help your student teachers to identify those areas of their practice they wish to develop in a number of ways. One is by getting them to 'step back' from their classroom practice and reflect generally on their aspirations as teachers. The following kinds of questions can be helpful:

- Why did you decide to enter teaching?

- What do you want to achieve?

- How do you define your role as a teacher?

- How do you see the job of teaching?

- What kind of teacher do you want to be?

Having identified these very broad concerns – a desire to enthuse all pupils about the subject, for example, or a commitment to achieving social justice in their teaching – your student teachers can then be encouraged to relate the general aim back to classroom practice and to think about specific ways in which that aim can be translated into teacher actions.

EXAMPLE Translating broad aims into specific targets

1. A history student teacher had entered teaching because of a love of her subject and above all wanted to pass on her enthusiasm to young people. Through discussion with her mentor about ways of motivating pupils, she decided to concentrate on lesson introductions. The questions she asked about her own practice focused on the effectiveness of her use of language, variety of tone and pace, and movement. She experimented with a range of activities to generate pupil interest in a new topic.

continued overleaf

> *2. A maths student teacher's commitment to 'social justice' was expressed in a concern that quiet pupils should receive as much individual attention and help as the more vocal and often less well-behaved members of the class.*

For some student teachers the process works in reverse. The area of interest develops from something they have actually experienced in their teaching. Even when the specific focus is identified first it will obviously be influenced by the broader view of teaching held by the student teacher, who must be able to explain why he or she believes it to be a valid concern, worthy of detailed analysis.

Student teachers may, however, identify the specific focus first as it often arises through diagnostic assessment or out of particular difficulties they experienced during the first phase.

EXAMPLE   Further work arising from a previous difficulty

1. A geography student teacher had been particularly struck by a debriefing session with her mentor during the first phase of her teaching, in which they had focused on one aspect of the agreed list of teaching qualities/ competences/skills: 'Are pupils positively involved in the lesson?' Her consideration of this issue led her to question whether she was providing appropriate extension activities for the more able pupils, since the disruptive elements in the classroom tended to be those who finished tasks early. A concern to meet the needs of all pupils, including the most able, became the focus of her self-evaluation.

2. A science student teacher who decided to explore her use of language – whether scientific terms she used in the lesson were understood by the pupils – selected this as the focus for her self-evaluation on the basis of comments made by the university tutor observing one of her lessons quite early in her time in school. She had become fascinated by this aspect of her work and welcomed the opportunity afforded to explore the issue of pupil understanding of terms used routinely by teachers.

Changing relationships: difficulties and temptations

Your role in observing student teachers is to provide them with objective data – evidence about their teaching – which they can use in forming judgements of their own effectiveness. It is not for you to pass judgement on how well they performed in the classroom.

Yet your role is not confined simply to that of collecting data, handing them to the student teachers and leaving them to make sense of them alone. Self-evaluation is not easy: it demands not only a willingness to ask critical questions about one's own practice and a determination to improve, but an understanding of what questions are important to ask. It is asking too much of student teachers to expect them to carry out that task alone. You have a crucial role to play in:

- prompting the student teachers to ask certain questions
- challenging them to substantiate their conclusions
- pointing out to them the data they might otherwise overlook
- encouraging them to recognize the implications of their answers.

The new relationship between you and the student teachers that this requires is demanding. Supporting your student teachers as they take responsibility for evaluating their own performance is difficult because:

- student teachers value your opinion and tend to ask for it
- as mentor you are often tempted to offer an opinion
- student teachers may fall below an acceptable standard of competence
- it can seem easier to allow student teachers simply to get on with it.

Student teachers value your opinion
However good the relationship between you and your student teachers, transition from assessor to partner in the learning process is not an easy one for either of you. As mentor, you are used to making value judgements and most student teachers still look for encouragement or even criticism, valuing what they regard as authoritative judgements about their teaching. At the end of a lesson, most student teachers still seek some kind of reassurance that everything was basically 'OK', and when analysing the lesson in detail it would be surprising if they did not continue to seek your opinion as a respected professional.

The temptation to pass judgement
Even when not directly asked, it is hard not to express an opinion. The difficulty of refraining from making judgements when impressed with the observed teaching is illustrated by the experience of an established mentor:

EXAMPLE The desire to praise

I'd been asked by my student to focus on the way she used her voice in the lesson, something we both felt she needed to work on. During the lesson I was really pleased to see how much progress Susan (the student teacher) had made and I found myself writing down notes such as: 'excellent use of tone to emphasise key words' and 'real improvement – much slower and clearer' which certainly wasn't going to help her learn how to judge her work for herself. I found that I had to discipline myself to make sure that I described what happened as objectively as possible.

Equally, you as mentor may personally feel very critical of a particular strategy adopted by a student teacher or believe that the student teacher has clearly failed to meet his or her objectives. After taking responsibility for the student teacher's learning for so long it can be very difficult to refrain from commenting negatively rather than to respect the student teacher's judgement.

Student teachers' loss of competence

The problem is compounded by the fact that student teachers can and sometimes do slip back in terms of basic competence. There may be occasions (albeit very rarely) when either in respect of the agreed focus of the observation, or in other respects, a student teacher teaches in a way that can only be described as falling below the standard of basic competence. Clearly you cannot let this pass, and the fact that a student teacher has moved into a new phase does not give them licence to jettison the agreed list of qualities/competences/skills. This phase is an opportunity for student teachers to develop their own teaching skills without the constant worry of whether or not they will 'pass the test'. However, the standard is not then abandoned.

There is thus a tension in your role: the need to refrain from passing value judgements in order to allow the student teachers to evaluate their own performance often goes against the natural inclinations of both you and student teachers. It requires a new relationship. Yet the relationship cannot be entirely transformed, for on rare occasions you may have to act again as judge of student teachers' basic competence.

The demands of self-evaluation

To cope with the transition you may be tempted, rather than passing judgement, to move to the opposite extreme, which unfortunately can be even more unhelpful in terms of the student teachers' learning. Accepting that the student teachers are now responsible for evaluating their own performance, you may step right back, confining your role to the collection of data requested by the student teachers, leaving them to assess their significance. This temptation to leave student teachers simply to get on with it is especially strong when they are clearly very competent and everything seems to be going well. This would not only be a considerable waste of your expertise, but would present the student teacher with an almost impossible task.

Evaluating one's own performance is extremely demanding even for experienced teachers and you as mentor have a vital role in helping student teachers *learn* how to do it. You need to ask questions to help the student teachers develop an understanding of the kind of questions they should be asking of the data presented to them. This is the case even where things are going well. Success in teaching is often much more difficult to analyse than failure, and it is precisely because a particular strategy seems to have worked that the student teachers will require more help in analysing the reasons for its success than they would have needed in explaining why it failed!

Partnership supervision – putting it into practice

Pre-lesson discussion

Before a particular lesson is observed, you and the student teacher will still need to meet briefly to clarify exactly what the focus of your observation is to be, and to agree on:

- how you will observe the lesson
  - sitting at the back
  - working with a small group
  - focusing on an individual
- what data you will collect
- the wording of any observation schedule
- arrangements for post-lesson discussion.

Observation and data collection

There are two sorts of information which it may be helpful for you to collect – one focuses on the student teacher and the other on the pupils in the lesson.

EXAMPLE Collecting data about the student teacher's actions

A science student teacher concerned about her use of language asked her mentor to record, as far as possible verbatim, the explanation she gave when she first introduced a new scientific term.

EXAMPLE Observing pupils' responses

A geography student teacher, analysing how well she motivated and stretched the more able pupils in the class, asked her mentor to monitor two specific pupils and note at five-minute intervals exactly what each was doing. On the first occasion the two pupils were selected by the student teacher; on the second they were to be selected by the mentor.

If your student teacher provides you with an observation schedule setting out exactly what they would like you to look at, and how they would like the evidence to be recorded, it is worth checking that:

- the meaning of the questions or headings is clear

- the questions are appropriate

- the student teacher can explain how the answers to these questions are likely to prove useful

- the questions do not in fact require the observer to make value judgements.

For example, for a student teacher to ask, 'Does "X" seem appropriate?' would be to invite his or her mentor to make a value judgement and would therefore be inappropriate. Figure 7.1 is an example of a student teacher's observation schedule, with notes made by the mentor while observing the lesson. Note that the questions ask for objective responses rather than subjective judgements, and that the mentor's jottings are a record of what she observed rather than what she felt about the lesson.

Depending on the focus of the self-evaluation it may not be necessary for you to observe the whole lesson; a student teacher investigating, say, the effectiveness of her introductions only needs information collected about the first part of the lesson and there is no need for the mentor to stay beyond this point.

Any notes that you write while observing the lesson will therefore, as far as possible, be factual and non-judgemental, as in Figure 7.1. They should contain statements about what and when things were done, rather than how well or why they were perceived to be done.

Debriefing

It is useful to follow a broad set pattern that reflects the new relationship in partnership supervision as shown in Figure 7.2.

Figure 7.1 *Example of an observation schedule devised by a student teacher*

Focus of self-evaluation: Capturing pupils' interest at the beginning of lessons/new topics

Date *12th May*

Class *7C*

Lesson Topic *"Register" - different sorts of language*

1. Please note down (as far as possible) my first few words to the class introducing the lesson. *Put up your hand if when you're with your friends or mates you speak differently - different words, perhaps different kinds of sentences, even different accents - from the way you speak, say, with a teacher.*

2. What type of teaching activity was used to introduce the lesson? *Opening question, repeated & rephrased, followed by 3 examples drawn from pupils using question & answer. Linking explanation - from their use of variety of language → collection of tapes. Notion of "register" introduced.*

3. Describe, as far as possible, my gestures, tone of voice and movement around the room during the introduction. *At front for opening question - moved towards the individuals you asked to explain their examples. Clicked fingers - pointed when asking Sue for her example (as well as using her name). During playing of tape sitting at front (no movement) sounded enthusiastic with key words emphasised.*

4. What was required of the pupils during the introduction?
   1. Respond by putting hands up.
   2. Individuals (3) required to offer examples.
   3. Listen to tape & make notes about the different uses of language.

5. Describe the pupils' response – their gestures, tone of voice and any movement. *No pupil movement - except heads turned to look at individual talking to class. Very attentive during playing of tape. All pupils jotting notes. Initial hesitation when opening question first posed - once question was rephrased one or two pupils waving hands & several cries of 'Miss, Miss' suggesting enthusiasm to answer, and many with hands up.*

6. How long was the introduction? *15 minutes, including tape extracts.*

Figure 7.2 *Shaping the debriefing*

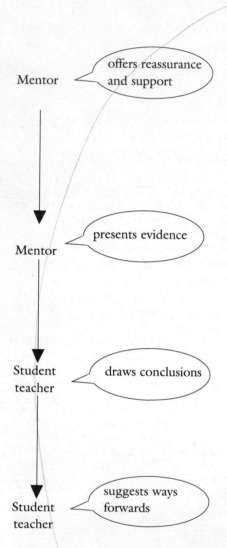

Mentor — offers reassurance and support

Before formal discussion can begin you will probably need to offer a word of encouragement to the student teacher, and it would be heartless and almost impossible not to do so. However, this should be *brief* and expressed in general terms, and not stand in the way of the student teacher developing their own balanced judgement.

Mentor — presents evidence

In explaining the evidence you again must try to remain non-judgemental, simply clarifying what you have written, as necessary.

Student teacher — draws conclusions

The onus here is on the student teacher, but it is your questions that will help the student teacher to do this effectively.

Student teacher — suggests ways forwards

Here too your questions play a vital role.

The kind of questions that you might ask to help the student teacher draw conclusions are:

- Is that the outcome you expected when you planned the strategy?

- How might you explain the pupils' response to the question?

- Why do you think that happened?

- How does this compare with what happened last lesson? Can you suggest reasons for the difference?

And in helping them to suggest ways forward:

- Given the difficulties the pupils seemed to have, how would you adapt that task?

- Are there ways in which you would alter the introduction in the light of this evidence?

The importance of your questions in helping student teachers to analyse their teaching can be seen in the following extract from a debriefing conversation. It took place after the lesson referred to earlier (Figure 7.1) when the mentor had been asked to complete an observation schedule that focused on introductions.

EXAMPLE Skilful probing

Mentor: So, in the light of all that, (the observation schedule) what do you feel about your tone of voice and use of gestures?

Student: I don't know what to say really.

Mentor: Compare it with the Year 10 class I saw you with last week.

Student: I think I'm more dramatic with Year 7 than with upper groups like Year 10. Maybe that's something I should try to do more with upper groups.

Mentor: Why do you think that is?

Student: With Year 7, they're actually waiting to see what you're going to do. They want to know what you're going to do, and how the lesson's going to start. With Year 10, they're not so bothered. More of a curiosity factor with Year 7 and maybe that encourages me to be a bit more excited.

Mentor: So you think it's to do with their age, and enthusiasm? And so perhaps you feel more confident with them, is that it?

Student: Yes, so gestures and tone of voice are still something I need to think more about with the Year 10 class. There's not been a definite starting point with them as there is with this group.

Mentor: What do you mean by a definite starting point?

Student: This group all line up and wait outside for me. I bring them in and I start the lesson, and it's obvious when the lesson starts.

Mentor: And, with Year 10?

Student: Well, that's different. They don't wait outside because they're older – they sort of drift in and I start the lesson when I think they're all there. But there isn't the same sort of feeling of starting-off – it's all a bit vague.

Mentor: So how do you think you could create that same sense of anticipation for Year 10, and grab their attention?

As the student teachers begin to suggest ways forward you may have ideas of your own to put forward, but it is important that the student teachers' thinking comes first, and that any suggestions that you make are evaluated by them in the light of what they have learned. The student teachers are still likely to want to know what you actually thought of what they did. Your opinion, as that of a respected professional, can be given, but only *after* they have done their own thinking.

The focus of a student teacher's self-evaluation may be a comparison of the effectiveness of different strategies with the same group for example, so the point of some post-lesson discussions may be simply to analyse the effectiveness of the approach used on that occasion, and not necessarily to suggest future improvements. However it is important that at certain stages within the process of self-evaluation you help student teachers to articulate not only what they have learned but how it will influence their future practice.

You may find it valuable to divide the discussion into two parts with some time between your explanation of the evidence and the student teachers' evaluation of it. This will allow the student teachers time to reflect on the evidence and begin to develop their own conclusions from it, thus ensuring a more fruitful discussion.

COLLEAGUES WORKING WITH STUDENT TEACHERS

As with assessment, colleagues in your department are also likely to be involved in observing student teachers teaching during the second phase. Part of your role therefore is to ensure that they understand the basic difference between the two phases and are confident about the process of partnership supervision.

Summary

Self-evaluation takes place in the second phase of the student teachers' learning, once they have been judged to be competent teachers. Your role as mentor within the process involves helping the student teachers:

- *identify the area of interest on which they wish to work*

- *evaluate their own teaching through partnership supervision.*

Partnership supervision involves:

- *pre-lesson discussion*

- *observation and data-collection*

- *debriefing.*

To do it well you need to:

- *give the student teachers appropriate reassurance and support without passing judgement*

- *enable the student teachers to make their own judgements, without abandoning them.*

INDEX